chattering cl

D0895787

RELIGIOUS HOSTILITY

A Global Assessment of Hatred and Terror

Rodney Stark and Katie E. Corcoran

ISR BOOKS

Cover designed by Barbara E. Williams, BW&A Books, Inc.
Art by imagedepotpro/Collection E+/Getty Images
Proofread by Dorothy Chambers
Packaged by Wish Publishing

Printed in the United States of America
10 9 8 7 6 5 4 3 2

Published by ISR Books
One Bear Place #97236
Baylor University
Waco, TX 76798

Table of Contents

Preface

This is the first in a projected series of monographs by members of the Institute for Studies of Religion at Baylor University. Launched in 2004, ISR exists to initiate, support, and conduct research on religion, involving scholars and projects spanning the academic spectrum: history, sociology, economics, anthropology, political science, psychology, epidemiology, theology, and religious studies. Our mandate extends to all religions, everywhere, and throughout history. While always striving for appropriate scientific objectivity, our scholars treat religion with the respect that sacred matters require and deserve.

Introduction: The New Religious Wars

July 4, 2013: Once again Egyptians are killing one another. Once again the army has deposed the government—this one having been a freely elected tyranny. Once again the Western press is hopeful that out of this turmoil will come a secular regime that will end the reign of religious brutality in Egypt. And once again there seems to be no awareness that Egyptians are overwhelmingly opposed to any such regime—that two out of three want the country to be ruled *entirely* in accord with Shari'a (orthodox Muslim law), and only 2 percent want a secular legal system. The army might install what appears to be a secular government, but if it truly is secular, it will never be popular and will endure only so long as the army imposes it. For Egypt is among the most orthodox of Muslim nations, far more like Saudi Arabia and Pakistan than like its North African neighbors, Libya, Tunisia, Algeria, or Morocco. As will be seen, nine out of ten Egyptians favor the death penalty for all Muslims who convert to another religion, and four out of ten approve of "honor killing" female relatives suspected of misbehavior.

That's why we wrote this book—to impose the discipline of real data on discussions of worldwide religious hostility. How many people are dying because of their faith? Where? Killed by whom? Why? And what about angry atheists and the extent of anti-atheism? How many and in which nations welcome terrorism and extremism? What role are governments playing in all this? Is there a new Christian exodus? Are Jews fleeing Western Europe? Is religious civility possible? We shall see.

On the Battlefield

More than twenty years ago, Samuel Huntington predicted that religion would become the primary basis for conflict in the post-Cold War world.[1] And so it has come to be, but with an important difference. In earlier times, religious wars were fought by armies. Today they are mainly fought by civilian ✳ volunteers.

Although religious atrocities occur in many parts of the world, the primary battlefield is in the Islamic nations or where there is a militant Muslim minority. The wars take many forms.

Attacks by small squads of terrorists.

- *Nigeria*. December 12, 2012: Fifteen Christian women and children are tied up inside a church, and their throats are slit by men shouting praises to Allah.

- *Algeria*. December 12, 2012: A Muslim imam is stabbed to death after denouncing Islamic extremism.

- *Pakistan*. November 11, 2012: Six Sunni seminary students are machine-gunned by Shi'ah militants in a tea shop.

- *Somalia*. November 16, 2012: A young Muslim, accused of being a secret Christian, is dragged into the street by activists and beheaded before a crowd of his neighbors, who cheer as his body is split into two and carried away.

- *Pakistan*. December 18, 2012: A women administering polio vaccine to children is shot dead by militants who believe this is a Western plot against Islam.

- *Thailand*. February 5, 2013: Four Buddhist merchants are tied up and slaughtered by a Muslim squad.

- *Egypt*. April 7, 2013: Two Christians are killed and eighty-six are injured when Muslim radicals attack a group of mourners leaving a Coptic church.

- *United Kingdom*. May 22, 2013: Two Nigerian Muslims attack a British soldier with knives and a meat cleaver and behead him on a street in London. When taken into custody, one of the terrorists shouts, "We swear by Almighty Allah we will never stop fighting you."

- *Pakistan.* June 15, 2013: Militants opposed to education for women blow up a bus carrying female university students, leaving twenty-three dead. A suicide bomber then strikes the medical center where student survivors are being treated, followed by gunmen using rockets and grenades. Seven more, including four nurses, are killed.

- *Syria.* June 23, 2013: Muslim militants kidnap a Roman Catholic priest and then behead him with an ordinary carving knife while a large crowd watches and cheers. Dozens of the onlookers photograph the event with their cell phones, and some of these photos are then placed triumphantly on the Internet.

Atrocities by angry mobs.

- *Palestinian Territory.* November 20, 2012: Six "unbelievers" are tortured and killed by a Hamas mob, their bodies dragged through the streets behind motorcycles.

- *Bangladesh.* February 19, 2013: A young boy is burned alive during a rampage by a Muslim mob through a Hindu village.

- *Pakistan.* March 3, 2013: A Muslim mob rampages through a Christian neighborhood, burning more than 100 homes and injuring dozens.

- *Egypt.* April 6, 2013: A Muslim mob outraged over an alleged "desecration" burns a Christian church, killing seven worshippers.

- *China.* April 23, 2013: Six policemen and nine civilians are hacked and burned to death by an enraged mob of Muslims.

- *Myanmar.* May 2, 2013. One Muslim is killed and ten are injured as a Buddhist mob attacks two mosques and burns Muslim neighborhoods.

Murders by individuals who explode suicide vests or set off bombs in order to destroy sinners and heretics.

- *Afghanistan*. May 3, 2013: Fifty-three people die and more than 100 are injured when nine Muslim radicals self-detonate in a crowded courtroom.

- *Somalia*. February 8, 2012: Fifteen people sitting in a hotel café are torn to shreds by a Fedayeen suicide bomber.

- *Kenya*. April 4, 2013: Al-Shabaab Islamists throw a hand grenade into a restaurant, killing three.

- *United States*. April 15, 2013: Four Americans are killed and several hundred are wounded by bombs planted by two Muslim brothers at the finish line of the Boston Marathon.

- *Syria*. March 21, 2013: Forty-nine worshippers in a Sunni mosque are killed by a Shahid suicide bomber.

- *Nigeria*. March 18, 2013: Forty-one Christians are killed by a suicide car bomber.

- *Pakistan*. March 9, 2013: Six Sufis die when Sunni Muslims explode a bomb in their mosque.

- *Iraq*. February 28, 2013: Sunni extremists set off a car bomb outside a crowded Shi'ah restaurant, killing eleven.

- *India*. February 17, 2013: Seventeen Hindus are killed by a bomb planted by Muslim Mujahedeen.

Acts by fanatics who murder their neighbors and associates.

- *Tajikistan*. January 2, 2012: A Christian who dressed up as Father Christmas for a children's party is stabbed to death by his neighbors as an "infidel."

- *Ukraine*. October 20, 2012: Three young Muslims murder their Jewish professor.

- *Vietnam*. March 29, 2013. Buddhist villagers choose Good Friday to attack their Christian neighbors, beating the local pastor to death and injuring many worshippers.

Tragedies when families "honor kill" their daughters for alleged transgressions.

- *Turkey.* December 26, 2012: A young woman is strangled by her family to restore their honor in the wake of her having been raped by her cousins.

- *Pakistan.* October 31, 2012: A Muslim couple honor kill their daughter by dousing her in acid for speaking to a man.

- *Egypt.* June 11, 2012: A young girl is beaten by her brothers and then thrown to her death off a building when suspected of being in a "relationship."

- *Palestinian Territories.* February 14, 2012: A twenty-six-year-old woman is strangled by her mother over a rumor of sexual impropriety.

Actions by enraged individuals.

- *China.* March 7, 2013: A Muslim goes on a stabbing spree against unbelievers, killing five and wounding seven.

- *United States.* March 24, 2013: A young man who has converted to Islam enters a Christian church with Qur'an in hand and guns down his father while praising Allah.

- *Norway.* January 15, 2013: A Muslim stabs two converts from Islam to Christianity.

- *Egypt.* May 9, 2013: An American professor is stabbed five times in the neck by a college-educated Muslim extremist. Ironically, the professor is ardently pro-Muslim and violently anti-American.

In all, during the past decade there probably have been more than twenty thousand incidents such as these, and the total number of deaths probably exceeds 300,000.

Religious Versus Secular Conflicts

In Western nations the religious wars seldom involve bloodshed, being primarily conducted in the courts and legislative bodies. In these arenas, the battles are not usually between religions but between religious and secular interests, the latter often being ardently antireligious. Even the cases involving religious terrorism very often are confrontations between the religious and the irreligious.

Anti-Abortion Terrorism

why aside

In the United States, aside from acts of Muslim terrorism and those involving federal agents at Waco[2] and at Ruby Ridge,[3] nearly all lethal incidents have been religiously motivated attacks on abortionists.

- *March 10, 1993*: Dr. David Gunn of Pensacola, Florida, is fatally shot outside his clinic by Michael F. Griffin, who makes no attempt to flee. Griffin is now serving a life sentence.

- *July 29, 1994*: Dr. John Britton and his bodyguard are shot to death in Pensacola—Britton had replaced David Gunn as the local abortionist. Rev. Paul Jennings was convicted of the killings and executed.

- *December 30, 1994*: Two receptionists are shot to death and five people wounded by shootings at two Planned Parenthood clinics that performed abortions in Brookline, Massachusetts. John Salvi confessed to the killings and committed suicide in prison.

- *January 29, 1998*: An off-duty policeman employed as a security guard is killed when a bomb explodes at an abortion clinic in Birmingham, Alabama. Eric Robert Rudolph was convicted of the bombing and is serving two life sentences in prison.

- *October 23, 1998*: Dr. Barnett Slepian is shot to death by a high-powered rifle at his home in Amherst, New York. James Kopp was convicted of the killing after having been apprehended in France in 2001.

- May 31, 2009: Dr. George Tiller is shot and killed while serving as an usher at the Reformation Lutheran Church in Wichita, Kansas. Tiller was one of fewer than a dozen physicians in the nation who performed very-late-term abortions. Scott Roeder confessed to killing Tiller and is serving a life sentence.

How are these religiously motivated

In addition, since 1984 there have been fifteen attacks on abortion clinic buildings: seven arsons, four bombing attempts, one incident of vandalism with an axe, and three instances of a motor vehicle crashing into a clinic.

Anti-abortion terrorism has not been restricted to the United States. There have been two incidents in Australia.

- *July 16, 2001*: A security guard at an abortion clinic in Melbourne is shot and killed. His killer was caught and sentenced to life in prison.

- *January 6, 2009*: A clinic in western Australia is ineffectively firebombed, and graffiti reading "baby killers" is painted on the wall.

In New Zealand, a man is convicted of attempting to tunnel into an abortion clinic, apparently to place an explosive device.

In Canada, four attempts are made to assassinate abortionists, all of whom survive their wounds.

Suppressing Religious Expression

When Abraham Lincoln and his Secretary of the Treasury had "In God We Trust" put on American coins and currency, they were not ignorant of the First Amendment. They were fully aware that it guaranteed freedom *of* religion, that the "Congress shall make no law respecting the establishment of religion or prohibiting the free exercise thereof."

As the Founding Fathers who wrote and ratified the First Amendment understood the matter, this meant that Congress would not give official standing and tax support to any religious body, as was the practice in England and most of Europe and as had been the situation of the Anglican Church (now Episcopalian) in six of the thirteen colonies, and of the Congregational Church (Puritans) in the New England colonies—Massachusetts only ceased supporting the Congregational Church in 1833. The Founders did not understand the First Amendment to mean that the state must eschew all religious expression—although himself a skeptic, Benjamin Franklin proposed that all sessions of the Constitutional Convention be opened with a prayer. It occurred to no one that this was in any way improper. And that was how the First Amendment was understood for nearly two centuries.

Then came the utterly unprecedented (5 to 4) Supreme Court proclamation in 1947 in the case of *Everson v. Board of Education* that "the First Amendment has erected a wall between church and state. That must be kept high and impregnable. We must not approve the slightest breach." Subsequently, this ruling was expanded and reinforced with the result that today the courts are swamped with suits demanding what the plaintiffs openly proclaim as freedom *from* religion. Indeed, the name of one of the most active plaintiff groups is the Freedom From Religion Foundation (FFRF). On its home page, FFRF describes itself as "the nation's largest association of freethinkers (atheists, agnostics, and skeptics) with over 19,000 members." They make no secret of their hostility toward religion; their website displays a label to be placed on Bibles: "Warning! Literal Belief in this Book May Endanger Your Health and Life!"

- *February 1, 2013*: A suit is filed by FFRF against the United States Treasury for placing "In God We Trust" on currency.

- *May 30, 2012*: FFRF and a student sue a school district in South Carolina for permitting a prayer at graduation ceremonies.

- *August 14, 2012*: FFRF files suit in the U.S. District Court in Montana to require the U.S. Forest Service to no longer permit a shrine to Jesus in Flathead National Forest.

- *September 14, 2012*: FFRF and two parents sue a school district in Pennsylvania demanding removal of a monument displaying the Ten Commandments.

- *December 22, 2011*: FFRF and one of their local members sue Warren, Michigan, to cease allowing display of a nativity scene on public land.

And so it goes. The FFRF is only one of many similar groups devoted to suits to suppress religious expression.

Nevertheless, not even the most militant atheist or secularist groups in the United States would consider trying to censor sermons. But that's precisely what the thicket of "hate speech" and "blasphemy" laws that have accumulated in Europe permit. When Sweden adopted a new hate speech statute in 2002, it explicitly included "church sermons" as subject to the law's provisions. A year later, a Swedish Pentecostal minister was sentenced to one month in prison for including Bible verses that condemn homosexual behavior in his Sunday sermon. Following this conviction, gay activists pledged to continue monitoring sermons and to report any new violations to authorities.

who is doing the persecuting

However, the primary focus of official enforcement of European hate laws has been to punish any comments about Islam deemed offensive to local Muslims.

- *The Netherlands*. 2009: Geert Wilders, member of the Dutch parliament and leader of its third largest political party, is indicted by a Dutch court for insulting Islam in remarks made about the growing Muslim presence in Europe and for his criticisms of Muslim terrorism. A month later, British officials deny Wilders admission to Great Britain on grounds that he is "a threat to the public order and public harmony." After years of legal hearings, Wilders is acquitted in 2011.

- *Denmark*. 2010: Jesper Marquand Langballe, a retired Lutheran minister and member of the Danish parliament, is convicted of libel and incitement to hatred toward Muslims for saying such things as "If Islamization is allowed to go on unhindered in Denmark, there is definitely a risk that in a few years we are subjected to Shari'a [Muslim law]." The next year, Lars Hedegaard, a well-known journalist, is convicted of hate speech for remarks criticizing the Muslim practice of honor killing by families of daughters suspected of not being virgins. In 2012 the Danish Supreme Court acquits Hadegaard. Then, on February 5, 2013, an unknown gunman attempts to shoot Hadegaard in his home.

  was he charged

- *France*. 2005: Jean Marie Le Pen, runner-up in the 2002 French presidential election, is convicted of inciting racial hatred for comments made to the press about the unpleasant consequences that are likely if Muslim immigration into France results in their becoming the majority.

- *Great Britain.* 2009: A couple in Liverpool are charged with causing harassment, alarm, or distress when a Muslim woman complains to police that the couple had told her Muslim dress codes are unfair to women.

Admittedly, European blasphemy laws are mild compared with those in Muslim nations. Pakistan's current law reads: "Whoever by words, either spoken or written, or by visible representation, or by imputation, innuendo, or insinuation, directly or indirectly defiles the sacred name of the Holy prophet Mohammed…shall be punished with death. …" Pakistan is not alone in having a draconian blasphemy law. To the extent that any Muslim nation honors Shari'a—the moral code and religious law of Islam—it imposes severe penalties of blasphemy. Soon after he was elected President of Egypt in 2012, Mohamed Morsi reaffirmed the death penalty for blasphemy, and seven Egyptian Christians were quickly tried and convicted. The Kuwait parliament recently passed a new law making blasphemy punishable by death, as it is in Afghanistan, Saudi Arabia, Yemen, and Iran. Slightly more "liberal" Muslim states such as Algeria, Jordan, and Indonesia limit the penalty for blasphemy to fines and imprisonment.

People and Nations

In the chapters that follow, we assess religious hostility around the globe. We shall do so at two levels, comparing people and comparing nations. To see how individuals of different religions and nationalities respond to questions about one another and about religious terrorism, we examine survey studies from most nations of the world. Here we will benefit from the remarkable Gallup World Poll studies—annual surveys of the adult population in each of 160 nations. A representative sample of at least one thousand adults is surveyed annually in each nation. Some questions of interest were asked in every nation, while other questions were asked in subsets of nations. These Gallup World Poll surveys were first conducted in 2005, so the samples for each nation can be combined to create a very large case base for analysis, such as comparing people of different religions within nations. We are indebted to the Gallup Organization for allowing us access to their database.

In addition, we will be able to draw on two other extremely valuable sets of international surveys. One of these is known as the World Values Surveys. These are conducted periodically in a number of nations under the direction of Ronald Inglehart of the University of Michigan. The World Values Surveys began in 1990 with twenty-four nations included and have been conducted approximately every five years since— the 2005-08 surveys included fifty-seven countries. The same items are asked in each nation (except when an item is excluded by local officials). The database for the World Values Surveys is freely available. A second set of worldwide surveys is known as the International Social Survey Program (ISSP), initiated and supervised by the National Opinion Research Center at the University of Chicago. The ISSP began in 1984 with surveys of four nations. Today, forty-nine nations participate. These data also are freely available to researchers. Finally, some fine international studies of religion and religious conflict have been conducted and published by Pew Foundation. We shall augment our statistical analysis by comparisons with Pew's published findings.

Beyond examining data on individuals, we will also compare nations. Where are levels of religious prejudice and hostility highest? Which nations suffer most from religious atrocities? To what degree do nations differ in sustaining religious liberty and freedom? Which governments persecute religious nonconformity? And what are the trends—are the religious wars waxing or waning? But first, it will be useful to examine an up-to-date religious portrait of the world.

Chapter One:
Faiths on Earth

Worldwide religious statistics are based on a substantial amount of guesswork.[1] While some nations have reliable counts of their religious make-up, many do not, and therefore all of the previously available statistics on worldwide religious affiliation are rough estimates. They also include very nominal "members" of all the major faiths. Thus, for example, nearly everyone in Europe is included in the Christian total, even though many European "Christians" have never been inside a church and many others have only been there once, when they were baptized as infants. By the same token, everyone living in some Muslim nations is counted in calculations of Islamic membership, but even in these countries some Muslims never visit a mosque.

Far more accurate estimates of religious affiliation now can be calculated based on data from the Gallup Organization's World Poll. As already noted, since 2005 Gallup has conducted annual surveys in each of 160 nations having about 97 percent of the world's population. Respondents are asked, "Could you tell me what your religion is?" In addition, Gallup asks, "Have you attended a place of worship or religious service within the past seven days?" Of course, these questions were carefully translated into all of the local languages. Hence, in principle, the data from these surveys can provide an accurate and far more informative portrait of the world's religions.

However, there are several unavoidable shortcomings, even to these revised statistics. In many nations, respondents are given the choice of affirming they are Roman Catholics, Protestants, or Orthodox Christians. But in many places, although people know the name of their local Christian church, they are unfamiliar with terms such as Protestant or Catholic. Consequently, in many countries it was necessary to settle for the response "Christian," without further specification. Hence, to create worldwide statistics, even those who reported being Protestant, Catholic, or Orthodox must be placed in the undifferentiated category, "Christian." The same applies to Muslim respondents. For many nations there is no breakdown even for Sunnis and Shi'ah, and hence everyone is simply identified as a "Muslim."

A second deficiency is that even though by now there are about a million respondents to the World Polls, there still are too few cases to allow reliable statistics to be computed for some smaller religions, including Shinto, Zoroastrianism, Taoism, and Confucianism. This made it necessary to combine these, and all other small religions, into a hodge-podge category called "Other." In the next several years, as the size of the world sample increases, it will be possible to break down the "Other" category. In addition, there are those people who said they had no religion, or who responded they were secular, or atheists, or agnostics. All of these respondents were collapsed into the category, "Secular." However, millions of these "secular" people said they attended religious services in the past week!

A final difficulty arises because the Chinese government does not allow Gallup, or any other foreign polling agency, to ask questions about religious membership. Consequently, our statistics omit China. This is not as unfortunate as might be supposed, because most Chinese have very odd notions about what constitutes a religion. For example, most Chinese who frequently visit temples where they pray to various statues of gods and offer them gifts of food, will say they have no religion.[2] In addition, many Chinese who are active Buddhists or Christians will not admit that to strangers, including survey interviewers.[3] And for good reason, given the Chinese government's past record of religious persecution. In any event, although Christianity is growing quite rapidly in China,[4] and there has been a considerable revival of Chinese Buddhism,[5] the lack of World Poll data requires us to omit China from our statistics.

Nominal Members

Table 1-1 shows the membership of the great world religions outside of China. Around the world, a total of 2.1 billion people (40 percent) give their religion as Christian, far outnumbering Muslims, who total 1.4 billion (27 percent). Hindus are the third largest religious group, with one billion affiliates (19 percent), followed by Buddhists with 289 million (5 percent). Jews make up only thirteen million (less than 0.3 percent) and the other faiths number 116 million (2 percent). Secularists make up 295 million (6 percent).

Table 1-1: WorldWide Nominal Religious Affiliations (China Excluded)

	Number	Percent
Christians	2,177,871,000	40
Muslims	1,477,947,000	27
Hindus	1,046,389,000	19
Buddhists	269,302,000	5
Jews	13,106,000	0.3
Others	116,840,000	2
Secular	295, 683,000	6
TOTAL	5,397,138,000	99.3*

*Total less than 100 due to rounding error.

The major difference between these statistics and those most commonly cited has to do with the Secular category. This group usually is estimated at about 16 percent of the world population, a percentage that probably is obtained only by including most Chinese as unreligious. Inflating the Secular category causes a corresponding decrease in all the others, hence the proportion who are Christian usually is set at about 33 percent and Muslim at 21. That emphasizes why it is prudent not to include China. Be that as it may, these findings are very unsatisfactory in other ways.

Active Membership

What does it mean to be a Christian or a Muslim or a member of any faith? Surely it implies some degree of involvement and participation. The available measure of active membership is very stringent: "Have you attended a place of worship or religious service within the past seven days?" Table 1-2 is limited to those who attended in the past week.

Table 1-2: WorldWide Active Religious Affiliations (China Excluded)

	Number	Percent	Percent Reduction
Christians	1,166,751,000	39	46
Muslims	941,394,000	31	36
Hindus	686,351,000	23	34
Buddhists	143,042,000	5	47
Jews	3,153,000	*	76
Other	63,799,000	2	46
Secular	29,188,000	1	90
TOTAL	3,033,687,000	101**	45

* less than 0.1 percent
**Total percentage over 100 due to rounding error.

Contrary to stereotypes that all Muslims are ardent worshippers, their numbers have been reduced almost as greatly as those for Christians when the data are limited to weekly attenders. The table also reveals that more than twenty-nine million of those classified as Secular have attended a religious service in the past seven days! The overall finding is that nothing much has changed when only active members are examined. Christianity is still by far the largest of the religions (39 percent), followed by Islam (31 percent). However, in our judgment this is a more meaningful view of world religions than that based on nominal members.

Regionalism

Christianity is not only the largest religion in the world, it also is the least regionalized, as can be seen in Table 1-3. There are only trivial numbers of Muslims in the Western Hemisphere and in Eastern Asia, but there is no region without significant numbers of Christians. Even in the Arab region of the Middle

East and North Africa, 2 percent of the population are Christians—although this is probably only half as many as lived there a decade ago (see Chapter 7).

Table 1-3: Nominal Religious Affiliations by Regions (China Excluded)

	Christians	Muslims	Hindus	Buddhists	Jews	Other	Secular
North America	81%	*	*	*	2%	6%	10%
Latin America	93%	*	*	*	*	2%	4%
Europe	82%	5%	*	*	*	1%	12%
Middle East and North Africa	2%	96%	*	*	1%	*	*
Sub-Saharan Africa	66%	30%	*	*	*	3%	1%
South Central Asia	9%	31%	57%	2%	*	2%	1%
South Eastern Asia	21%	40%	1%	30%	*	2%	6%
Eastern Asia	15%	*	*	30%	*	6%	50%
Oceania	71%	2%	1%	1%	*	2%	21%

* less than 0.5 percent

Christian Regionalism

A more interesting way to examine Christian regionalism can be seen in Table 1-4.

Table 1-4: The Regional Distribution of Christians (China excluded)

	Nominal Affiliations	Weekly Attenders Only
North America	13%	12%
Latin America	25%	25%
Europe	23%	16%
Middle East and North Africa	*	*
Sub-Saharan Africa	24%	33%
South Central Asia	7%	4%
South Eastern Asia	6%	7%
Eastern Asia	1%	2%
Oceania	1%	*
TOTAL	100%	99%**

* less than 0.5 percent.
** Total percentage less than 100 due to rounding error.

There are some interesting surprises here. Christians are more likely to live in Latin America than elsewhere (25 percent), when only nominal affiliation is considered, with Sub-Saharan Africa (24 percent) and Europe (23 percent) close behind. But when the statistics are based on weekly church attenders, Europe (16 percent) falls to a distant third, and Sub-Saharan Africa rises to the top (33 percent). Despite the prominence of African bishops in the squabbles going on within the Anglican Communion, few know how highly Christianized is the entire subcontinent. This is further disguised by the common tendency to treat Africa as a whole rather than to divide it into the overwhelmingly Arab North and the Black South.[6] When treated as a united "continent," Africa has a Muslim majority. But that is very misleading, since Christians make up 66 percent of Sub-Saharan Africans, compared with 30 percent who are Muslims.

Christian Africa

The presence of so many Christians in Africa is not easily explained. Yes, Christianity reached these African communities as a result of European Colonialism—where the colonizers went, the missionaries followed. But it was taken for granted, both by Europeans and by African nationalists, that the collapse of European empires would quickly be followed by a return to precolonial, "authentically" African cultural forms. But nothing of the sort took place, at least not in the realm of religion. Instead, African Christianity has continued to thrive to such an extent that when only Christians who attend church weekly are counted, as already noted, there are more Christians in this part of Africa than anywhere else on earth.

An immense amount has been written about how this was brought about, with about equal stress placed on the immense number of Protestant missionaries stationed there and on the remarkable proliferation of thousands of African-born Protestant denominations. But these explanations have ignored the fact that at least 150 million of these African Christians are Roman Catholics. Thus, while there are more Protestants than Catholics in Sub-Saharan Africa, in many of these nations Catholics substantially outnumber Protestants. Thus, to write about the Christianization of Africa only in Protestant terms omits a major part of the story. Indeed, Catholic periodicals abound in reports of rapid growth in Africa, of substantial upward trends in the number of African priests and seminarians. In the twenty-year period of 1989-2009, according to official statistics, the number of priests in these Sub-Saharan nations rose from 16,580 to 30,339, and the number of seminarians surged from 10,305 to 25,162. This is a stunning achievement.

Islamic Regionalism

Muslims are bitterly opposed to Christian growth in Sub-Saharan Africa, and where Muslim and Christian areas abut, as in Nigeria, anti-Christian terrorism is rife. Thus, it may be fortunate that Muslims are more geographically concentrated than are Christians, as can be seen in Table 1-5.

Table 1-5: The Regional Distribution of Muslims (China excluded)

	Nominal Affiliations	Weekly Attenders Only
North America	*	*
Latin America	*	*
Europe	2%	1%
Middle East and North Africa	28%	24%
Sub-Saharan Africa	16%	19%
South Central Asia	38%	36%
South Eastern Asia	16%	20%
Eastern Asia	*	*
Oceania	*	*
TOTAL	100%	99%**

* less than 0.5 percent.
** Total percentage less than 100 due to rounding error.

Interestingly enough, the Arab nations of the Middle East and North Africa do not sustain the largest share of the Muslim population—more than a third live in the nations of South Central Asia, among them Afghanistan, Pakistan, Bangladesh, and India (there are more than 150 million Muslims in India). The substantial proportion of Muslims living in South Eastern Asia mainly reflects that Indonesia is the largest Islamic nation in the world. There are trivial numbers of Muslims in the Western Hemisphere and not many in Europe, despite the conflicts that have arisen there from recent Muslim immigration.

Growth

In recent years, many experts predicted that Islam would soon pass Christianity to become the largest religious group in the world.[7] These projections were based on the fact that Muslims had much higher fertility rates than Christians, and this was not expected to change. But then, Muslim fertility began to decline rapidly. It already is well below replacement level in Iran, Syria, and Jordan, and the fertility rate for the world's Muslim population in general is expected to fall to replacement level within the next several years. Thus, it no longer is likely that Muslims will simply out-reproduce Christians. Moreover, Islam generates very little growth through conversions, while Christianity enjoys a very substantial conversion rate, especially in nations located in what our colleague Philip Jenkins[8] describes as the "global south"—Asia, Sub-Saharan Africa, and Latin America. And these conversions do not include the millions of converts being gained in China.

Thus, current growth trends project an increasingly Christian world—even if Europe continues to slide into secularity. And that may not happen because of the remarkably different fertility of active and inactive Christians. While all of the Western European nations currently have fertility rates far below replacement levels, Europeans who are active Christian church members sustain fertility rates well above replacement level.[9] Should these differences persist, and if the children of religious Christians tend to remain religious, then Western Europeans will increasingly be made up of active Christians.[10] Meanwhile, because Muslim fertility has dropped rapidly in these European nations and continues to decline, any growth of Islam in Western Europe will depend on immigration. How this will influence the religious conflicts within these nations is hard to predict.

Conflict

Finally, what does the future hold for relations between the world's two largest religions? Recently, the Gallup World Poll asked people in many nations, "Do you think violent conflict between Islam and the Western worlds can be avoided or not?" Table 1-6 reports the results.

Table 1-6: Conflict Between the Muslim and Western Worlds

	Percent "Cannot Be Avoided"
North Africa and Middle East	
Afghanistan	23%
Algeria	41%
Azerbaijan	26%
Bahrain	52%
Bangladesh	24%
Egypt	48%
Iran	26%
Iraq	46%
Jordan	48%
Kuwait	43%
Lebanon	35%
Libya	39%
Morocco	14%
Pakistan	35%
Palestinian Territories	47%
Qatar	47%
Saudi Arabia	35%
Sudan	29%
Syria	31%
Tunisia	25%
Turkey	29%
United Arab Emirates	28%
Yemen	32%
Europe	
Albania	17%
Belgium	17%
Bosnia-Herzegovina	22%

Europe (cont.)	
Denmark	38%
France	15%
Germany	29%
Israel	48%
Italy	12%
Netherlands	27%
Norway	41%
Russia	14%
Spain	11%
Sweden	24%
United Kingdom	30%
Americas	
Brazil	17%
Canada	30%
United States	48%
Sub-Saharan Africa	
Burkina Faso	11%
Chad	31%
Comoros	23%
Djibouti	30%
Guinea	25%
Ivory Coast	9%
Mali	20%
Mauritania	24%
Niger	23%
Nigeria	29%
Senegal	10%
Sierra Leone	27%
Somaliland	42%
South Africa	45%
Tanzania	34%

Asia	
India	28%
Indonesia	15%
Japan	64%
Kazakhstan	5%
Malaysia	20%
Singapore	27%
Tajikistan	19%

This table could be interpreted several ways. One could be thankful that in nearly every nation, the majority thinks that violent conflict between the Muslim and Western worlds can be avoided. But one could also note that in most nations, a substantial minority thinks such a conflict cannot be avoided. Indeed, nearly half of Americans (48 percent) hold that violent conflict is unavoidable, as do the same percentage of Egyptians, Jordanians, and Israelis.

These are, of course, merely opinions. But, whatever else may lie ahead, it seems certain that hatred and terrorism will continue for years to come.

Chapter Two: Religious Atrocities

Every day the press reports new religious atrocities, stories of people murdered because of their religion. Until now, coverage of this global tragedy has been limited to reportage—to accounts of specific events such as those listed in the Introduction. But lists fail to give an adequate sense of what's going on. That requires summaries such as: How many thousands of people are dying annually? Where? Who? What groups are responsible for how many attacks and deaths?

Consequently, this chapter is based on our attempt to assemble a compendium of recent incidents of serious religious violence. Analysis of these cases will provide useful generalizations about the anatomy of religious atrocities.

Counting Religious Atrocities: 2012

The Internet offers many accounts of religious atrocities taking place around the world, including some remarkable efforts to assemble complete lists of various kinds of attacks.[1] We have drawn upon these sources to attempt to assemble a list of all attacks that occurred during 2012 that resulted in a fatality and that were motivated primarily by religious hostilities. However, we did not include violent incidents when they were perpetrated by government forces, such as army attacks on Christians or Muslims in Myanmar (Burma) or a Saudi Arabian police assault on a Shi'ah religious gathering. We also have excluded several thousand events for which religious motivation was not certain. Most of these involved Muslim extremists killing other Muslims, but unless the report included information that religious differences were of central concern, we did not include the incident. For example, on August 24, 2012, six people were killed when "Islamic terrorists" threw grenades into a hotel in Iraq. This may well have been motivated by religious antagonism, but it also could have been mainly a political matter, such as the desire to be rid of Americans, so we did not include it. On the other hand, when on August 27, 2012, Muslim extremists in Afghanistan broke into a party and beheaded two Muslim women and fifteen men for dancing to music, we did not hesitate to include this event in our compendium.

We also refused to be blinded by political correctness. Although the U.S. government has classified the Fort Hood murders, during which Major Nidal Malik Hasan shouted "Allahu akbar" while he gunned down his victims, merely as "workplace violence," we would not have hesitated to code it as a religious atrocity. So, too, when an Iranian recently chased a rabbi and his son through a Parisian synagogue and slashed them with a knife while also yelling "Allahu akbar," the Associated Press may have wondered as to his motive, but not us.

As we assembled the data, we became deeply concerned that nearly all of the cases we were finding involved Muslim attackers, and all the rest were Buddhists. We searched diligently for incidents involving attacks committed by Hindus, Jews, Christians, or, for that matter, atheists. We discovered a few involving Hindu attackers several years prior to 2012, but could find none for that year. Nor could we find any involving Jewish perpetrators during 2012. We truly ransacked all available sources in search of attacks by Christians. We thought we had one when we learned that on March 12, 2012 a mosque had been fire-bombed in Belgium and the imam had died of smoke inhalation. But the arsonist turned out to be a Salafi Muslim. We would, of course, have counted any of the cases wherein abortionists were murdered, had any occurred in 2012. But there were none. On August 15, 2012, a gunman did burst into the office of the Family Research Council in Washington, DC, and shoot a security guard, but no death occurred. Finally, we did find three incidents in Nigeria in which Christians killed Muslims, all three being reprisals for Muslim attacks on Christians, which have become commonplace in this large African nation.

What our search also revealed was the unsupported hysteria expressed by several self-styled experts on Christian terrorism. Sociologist Mark Juergensmeyer notes many "terrorists" who have done nothing whatever except hold beliefs that offend him.[2] In addition, he inappropriately identified Timothy

McVeigh, who committed the Oklahoma City bombing, as a Christian terrorist, although McVeigh never cited a religious reason for his act (only his antigovernment views) and was not personally religious at the time he blew up the building. As another instance, some have identified Randy Weaver as a Christian terrorist, even though the shoot-out at Ruby Ridge was, if anything, an attack by government terrorists, and Weaver was fully exonerated by the court and by the official investigation.[3] Juergensmeyer and others also charge that Anders Breivak, the Norwegian mass murderer, is a Christian terrorist. Granted that Breivak claimed he was defending Christian Norway against a Muslim takeover, but it seems reflective of his fundamental lunacy that his victims were mostly Lutherans and none of them Muslims. Of course, even if all these individuals were accepted to be Christian terrorists, their number is infinitesimal in the overall scheme of current religious atrocities.

In the end we assembled 810 incidents of religiously motivated homicides, in which 5,026 people died: 3,774 Muslims, 1,045 Christians, 110 Buddhists, 23 Jews, 21 Hindus, and 53 secular individuals. Keep in mind that these are very minimal estimates. Obviously, we could not discover all of the relevant cases, only those that were reported by the international press. Moreover, as noted, we observed very strict rules about what cases to count. Thus, even when people wearing explosive vests blew themselves up to kill others, we included the case *only* when there was a reported motive involving religious conflict—as when a Sunni Muslim blew himself or herself up among Shi'ah worshippers. Given that such acts of self-destruction seem comprehensible only on religious grounds, we considered among them, which would have added several hundred cases to our compendium. But we decided to stay with our restriction.

Table 2-1: Incidents of Religious Atrocities by Nation (2012)

Nation	Number of Incidents
Pakistan	267
Iraq	119
Nigeria	106
Thailand	52
Syria	44
Afghanistan	27
Yemen	22
India	20
Lebanon	20
Egypt	15
Somalia	14
Myanmar	11
Kenya	9
Russia	7
Sudan	7
Iran	6
Israel	6
Mali	6
Indonesia	5
Philippines	5
China	4
France	4
Libya	4

Nation	Number of Incidents
Palestinian	4
Algeria	2
Bangladesh	2
Belguim	2
Germany	2
Jordan	2
Macedonia	2
Saudi Arabia	2
Bahrain	1
Bulgaria	1
Kosovo	1
South Africa	1
Sri Lanka	1
Sweden	1
Tajikistan	1
Tanzania	1
Turkey	1
Uganda	1
TOTAL	810

Turning to the data, explosives (including firebombs) were used in 23 percent of the incidents. Firearms caused the deaths in 44 percent. In 9 percent, the killing was done with knives, and in 24 percent of the cases the victims were beaten and/or tortured to death. As to the latter, many of the incidents seem almost incomprehensible since they involved not a lone, demented sadist, but organized groups.

- *Yemen.* February 12, 2012: A man suspected of Christian sympathies is crucified and left to die slowly.

- *Syria.* March 25, 2012: An orthodox priest has his eyes gouged out and then is "horribly tortured" before being murdered.

Many other reports also tell of gouged-out eyes, of tongues torn out and testicles crushed, of rapes and beatings, all done prior to victims being burned to death, stoned, or slowly cut to pieces. Another barbaric twist is to make the primary victim watch while his or her loved ones are abused and murdered.

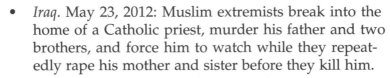

- *Iraq.* May 23, 2012: Muslim extremists break into the home of a Catholic priest, murder his father and two brothers, and force him to watch while they repeatedly rape his mother and sister before they kill him.

In contrast, car bombs and shootings seem almost humane.

Muslim Sectarianism

Notice that all three incidents above happened in Muslim nations. The fact is that for all of the concern in the West, especially in the United States, religious terrorism occurs almost exclusively *within* Islam. Of the 810 incidents we collected, 70 percent took place in Muslim nations—a third in Pakistan alone (see Table 2-1). In addition, 75 percent of the victims of religious atrocities during 2012 were Muslims killed by Muslims. All this is in keeping with the persistence of Muslim sectarianism.

The primary and most bitter division among Muslims arose soon after the death of Muhammad in 632 over who would become caliph ("successor") and take Muhammad's place. One faction favored Muhammad's cousin and son-in-law Ali. The other faction was sufficiently powerful to install Muhammad's old friend and father-in-law Abu-Bakr as caliph (Muhammad had at least eleven wives, so he had many in-laws). Abu-Bakr, in turn, appointed 'Unmar as his successor, again passing over Ali. Eventually this resulted in the Battle of Camel, which ended in the defeat of Ali's forces—he was subsequently assassinated. But this did not reunite Islam. Instead, Ali's supporters came to be known as the "Seceders" and have lived on as the *Shi'ah* (or Shi'ites), and the others became known as the *Sunni*. The Sunni are by far the larger group and are dominant in most Muslim nations, while the Shi'ah are the majority in Iran and Iraq. In addition, both the Shi'ah and the Sunni have produced many additional sects, including the Sufis, Wahhabis, Ahmadi, and Salafi. Relations among these groups remain so bitter that whenever official repression weakens, murderous conflicts erupt among them. And that is precisely why Pakistan suffers from such constant, bloody religious terrorism.

Pakistan has a Sunni majority, but about 20 percent of the population is Shi'ah. In addition, there are a substantial number of Ahmadi who believe that Mirza Ghulam Ahmad (1835-1908) was the promised Messiah. Both Sunni and Shi'ah bitterly reject the Ahmadi, and many support violent attacks upon them. And, of course, many Sunni and Shi'ah strongly support violent attacks on one another. In addition to all this, groups such as al-Qaeda and the Taliban make their own contributions to Pakistan's climate of religious terror. These are typical incidents, selected from many that took place in Pakistan during *one* month:

- December 30, 2012: Four Shi'ah, including a distinguished religious scholar, are beheaded by Sunni militants.

- December 20, 2012: A Sunni cleric is gunned down by Shi'ah.

- December 18, 2012: Sunnis detonate a car bomb outside a Shi'ah shrine, killing three.

- December 18, 2012: A Shi'ah doctor is murdered in his clinic by Sunni.

- December 4, 2012: A Shi'ah cleric and his four-year-old daughter are shot dead by Wahhabi gunmen.

- December 3, 2012: Taliban militants bomb two girls schools, killing several students.

- December 2, 2012: Sunni militants bomb a Shi'ah religious procession, killing two and injuring thirty-five.

As these incidents demonstrate, the Pakistani government has long been unable to suppress sectarian violence, even during its substantial periods of authoritarian military rule. In part, this is because those controlling the authoritarian regimes were themselves devoted to religious hatred and repression, while during periods of democratic rule, the parliament has been controlled by very doctrinaire Muslims. Thus, in 1974 the parliament officially declared the Ahmadis to not be Muslims, with the result that they lost many legal rights and became "fair game" for terrorists. To make matters worse, Saudi Arabia has long funded and educated Pakistan's Sunnis, causing them to become increasingly militant, while the Shi'ah have been funded and armed by Iran. Finally, the Taliban based next door in Afghanistan have gathered supporters in Pakistan as has al-Qaeda. And that's why Pakistan is Number One in religious atrocities.

In addition, Pakistan's Hindus, Christians, Jews and other "unbelievers" live under the constant threat of Pakistan's brutal law against blasphemy, quoted in the Introduction. Of course, in addition to vigorous legal enforcement stands mob action.

- December 22, 2012: A man accused of burning a Qur'an is dragged from a police station, tortured, beaten, and then set on fire by a mob.

- September 21, 2012: Two people are killed by a mob protesting a film about Muhammad.

- April 15, 2012: An eighty-year-old man is assassinated after being acquitted of blasphemy.

Killing Christians

As will be made clear in Chapter 6, our compendium does not include atrocities committed against Christians by government forces, which have sometimes involved hundreds of victims. Twenty percent (159) of the cases we compiled involved Christian victims, and of these, seventeen (11 percent) occurred in Pakistan. However, that total shrinks to insignificance compared with Nigeria, where half (seventy-nine) of all our recorded incidents involving Christian victims took place in 2012.

These incidents are very representative of Nigerian occurrences.

- December 25, 2012: Christmas services are interrupted by Boko Haram gunmen who kill the pastor and five worshippers.

- December 6, 2012: Boko Haram terrorists execute six Christians when they are unable to recite from the Qur'an.

- October 28, 2012: Seven worshippers are killed and about 100 injured when a Boko Haram suicide car bomber plows into a Catholic Church during mass.

- October 2, 2012: Twenty-six Christian students are singled out by Boko Haram militants who shoot some and cut the throats of the others.

Who are the Boko Haram?

They are Muslim extremists, whose formal name is Congregation and People of Tradition for Proselytism and Jihad. But they are better known by the name Boko Haram which, loosely translated from the Hausa language, means "Western education is forbidden." Indeed, in an interview with the BBC in 2009, the leader of Boko Haram denounced the notion that the earth is round as contrary to Islamic teaching.[4]

The Boko Haram movement was formed in 2002 by a popular Muslim cleric with the aim of imposing Muslim rule on all of Nigeria. The movement is based in the Muslim-dominated northeastern states of Nigeria and neighboring Cameroon. Many of its terror attacks are on government outposts, in pursuit of political domination. But even more often, Boko Haram atrocities are committed against Christians, who make up nearly half of Nigeria's population—Nigeria being the most populous nation in Africa, having about 170 million people. It is estimated that Boko Haram jihadists have killed more than 10,000 people in the past decade, many of them in drive-by shootings from the back of a speeding motorcycle. Boko Haram's anti-Christian jihad has attracted funding from abroad, especially from Saudi Arabia, and the group also seems to have links to al-Qaeda.

Of course, the Boko Haram were not the only terrorists dedicated to murdering Christians. There were fourteen such incidents in Syria, five in the Philippines, four in Egypt, and four in Somalia.

- *Syria.* December 31: A pregnant Christian woman is left a widow when Islamic extremists cut off her husband's head and feed it to dogs.

- *Syria*. November 16, 2012: Sunni raiders detonate a bomb outside an Orthodox church, killing twenty and injuring many more.

- *Syria*. August 29, 2012: A family of seven Christians, including three young children, are shot down in the street by radical Muslims.

- *Egypt*. June 29, 2012: Two Christians are murdered by Muslim Brotherhood activists.

- *Philippines*. July 22, 2012: Three Catholic priests are ambushed and murdered by Muslim gunmen.

- *Somalia*. January 2, 2012: A Christian humanitarian worker is beheaded by Muslim extremists.

- *Libya*. December 30, 2012: Muslim terrorists throw a hand grenade into a Coptic church, killing two.

Christian Terrorists

As already mentioned, all three incidents involving Christians killing Muslims occurred in Nigeria.

- January 6, 2012: Six Muslims are killed and seven are injured when young Christians attack a mosque and an Islamic school several days after a Boko Haram murder of eight Christians.

- November 18, 2012: A Muslim is shot dead after he fails to stop his car at a checkpoint set up to protect a Christian church.

- July 17, 2012: At least twenty Muslims are killed when angry bands of Christian youth drag Muslims from their cars and beat them to death following a suicide car bombing of two Christian churches.

Buddhist Victims

Seven percent (fifty-eight) of the incidents we counted involved Buddhist victims. Nearly all of these (76 percent) took place in Thailand. Here, Muslim religious terrorists are based in several provinces with a substantial Muslim population, although Thailand as a whole is more than 90 percent Buddhist. Some observers believe that the root cause is political, that the Muslim areas seek independence. That may be so, but most of the attacks are on individuals, not government outposts, and most have an ugly religious aspect.

- October 1, 2012: A Buddhist teacher is shot three times in the head by Muslim militants.

- September 21, 2012: Muslim terrorists detonate a car bomb outside a business that has remained open on an Islamic holy day, killing six and injuring more than forty.

- June 6, 2012: Muslim gunmen burn down a school and murder two teachers.

- May 13, 2012: Muslim terrorists throw grenades into a Red Cross fair, injuring more than twenty.

- February 5, 2012: Muslim terrorists open fire on a group of Buddhist monks, killing two.

In addition, Muslims in Thailand often kill other Muslims for failing to support jihad or for "heresies."

Hindu Deaths

Hindus were killed in twenty-three of the incidents we recorded, fifteen of them in India. Although most of the incidents in India involved Muslims killing Muslims, Muslim slayings of Hindus have a rather personal aspect.

- October 3, 2012: A Hindu boy is burned alive by angry Muslims for professing his love for a Muslim girl.

- September 5, 2012: A Hindu university student who spoke up about his religion in class is stabbed to death on campus by fellow Muslim students.

- July 18, 2012: Campus Muslims stab three Hindu students to death.

Death to the Jews

Eleven incidents involved Jewish deaths, only four of them in Israel.

- *Iran.* December 29, 2012: A Jewish man is murdered by a Muslim woman, whereupon the Iranian police congratulate her for doing "a good deed."

- *France.* March 12, 2012: A Muslim terrorist chases a rabbi and three children aged three, six, and ten, into a Jewish school in Toulouse and shoots all four of them to death.

- *Bulgaria.* July 18, 2012: A Shahid suicide bomber blows up an Israeli tourist bus, killing seven and injuring thirty.

Secular Victims

Finally, in twenty-eight of the incidents the victims' offense seemed not to lie in their religious identity, whatever it was, but in secular activities that were perceived as sinful or decadent.

- *Nigeria.* November 25, 2012: A tailor is killed by Boko Haram gunmen because he sewed clothing inappropriate for women to wear.

- *Nigeria.* November 10, 2012: Boko Haram shoot a refrigerator repairman to death in his shop—refrigerators being sinfully decadent.

- *Pakistan.* October 16, 2012: Taliban shoot a medical worker to death for vaccinating children, that program being regarded as a Western plot to "sterilize and poison" Muslim children. On May 28, 2013, after two more such shootings bring the total to twelve, the World Health Organization withdraws its polio vaccination teams.

- *Kenya.* July 30, 2012: Muslim terrorists murder a cell phone dealer.

- *Pakistan.* July 29, 2012: Extremists bomb a shop selling rock 'n roll CDs.

- *Egypt.* July 6, 2012: Muslim fundamentalists enter a pool hall and kill four players, having previously ordered the pool hall to close.

Fear of Extremists

Recently, the Pew Forum asked people in many nations "How concerned, if at all, are you about extremist religious groups in our country these days?"[5] Table 2-2 shows that all around the globe, Muslims are very or somewhat concerned about extremist religious groups—if not extremists from their own religious group, then those from rival sects. In Sub-Saharan Africa there were sufficient numbers of both Muslims and Christians in most nations to allow comparisons. Differences are small. It thus appears that religious violence concerns everyone.

Table 2-2: "How concerned, if at all, are you about extremist religious groups in our country these days?"

	Percent of Muslims who are Very or Somewhat Concerned
Middle East and North Africa	
Iraq	68%
Egypt	67%
Tunisia	67%
Palestinian Territories	65%
Morocco	62%
Lebanon	50%
Jordan	46%
Turkey	37%
Asia	
Indonesia	78%
Kazakhstan	63%
Malaysia	63%
Kyrgyzstan	62%
Pakistan	56%
Bangladesh	55%
Tajikistan	39%
Eastern Europe	
Bosnia and Herzegovina	63%
Russia	46%
Kosovo	45%
Albania	21%

	Percent of Muslims Who are Very or Somewhat Concerned	Percent of Christians Who are Very or Somewhat Concerned
Sub-Saharan Africa		
Botswana		53%
Cameroon	45%	45%
Chad	61%	61%
Congo (Democratic Republic of)	39%	50%
Dijibouti	49%	
Ethiopia	52%	66%
Ghana	62%	68%
Guinea Bissau	72%	79%
Kenya	57%	58%
Liberia	46%	61%
Mali	28%	28%
Mozambique	52%	51%
Niger	56%	
Nigeria	50%	51%
Rwanda	52%	56%
Senegal	21%	16%
South Africa		49%
Tanzania	46%	48%
Uganda	54%	45%
Zambia		61%

Islamophobia?

In the wake of the Boston Marathon bombing, sociologist Mark Juergensmeyer rushed into print to warn Americans not to blame religion, and certainly not the Islamic faith, for the actions of the Tsarnaev brothers.[6]

Although he has eagerly misidentified many as Christian terrorists, Juergensmeyer claimed the Tsarnaev brothers were "lone wolves"—they were not jihadists, but merely "angry young men." In similar fashion, Edward Said, the Palestinian-American Columbia University professor, claimed for years that Muslim terrorists are nothing but "a tiny band of crazed fanatics,"[7] for whom Islam bears no blame.

Unfortunately, efforts to deny any significant link between terrorism and Islam are not limited to a few professors. It is widespread, especially in the news media and current government circles. We already have noted the insistence that Major Hasan's murderous outburst at Fort Hood was not terrorism but "workplace violence." The words *Muslim* and *jihad* never appear in the official report on this incident (*Protecting the Force: Lessons from Fort Hood*), and the word *Islam* appears only once, in a footnote. In similar fashion, a study of terrorism issued by the Department of Homeland Security (*Evolution of the Terrorist Threat to the United States*) mentions Islam only once. And Attorney General Eric Holder, when testifying before Congress, absolutely refused to admit that the actions of various Muslim terrorists could be linked to religious motives. The underlying issue here has nothing much to do with who did what or why, but with the highly charged concept of Islamophobia.

The standard definition of Islamophobia is "prejudice against, hatred toward, or irrational fear of Muslims."[8] Leading proponents of this definition, most of whom apply it whenever any links are drawn between terrorism and Islamic radicalism, are primarily Western European intellectuals who participate in international commissions and forums, and leading Muslim spokespersons living in the West. And, of course, Islamophobia is enshrined in the many "hate speech" and "blasphemy" statutes that abound in Europe. Undoubtedly, some people are Islamophobic just as some are anti-Semitic and others hate Evangelical Christians. Trouble arises when the charge of Islamophobia is used to silence all comments on the obvious religious motivation of so many terrorists. Thus, in the aftermath of the public beheading of a British soldier on the streets of London by two Nigerian Muslims who proclaimed that they were acting to serve Allah, the highly respected *Manchester Guardian* headlined a local Muslim leader's denial: "These poor idiots have nothing to do with Islam." But, as the distinguished Ayaan Hirsi Ali pointed out in the *Wall Street Journal*,[9] in denying any connection between Islam and terrorism, Western Muslims leave themselves unable to debate claims by prominent Muslims in the Middle East who praise terrorists for doing their duty for Allah—Omar Bakri, a Muslim cleric living in Lebanon, said that the two who beheaded the British soldier were "courageous and brave...I don't see it as a crime as far as Islam is concerned."[10] Perhaps even worse is that concerns not to be guilty of Islamophobia have prevented some European government officials from acknowledging, let alone attempting to prevent, the increasingly frequent and serious attacks on their Jewish citizens by local Muslims, as will be seen in Chapter 7.

In any event, we are fully aware that millions of Muslims are not motivated by their faith to hate, let alone to kill those who do not fully share their religious outlook, and that many Muslim clerics teach that Islam is a religion of peace. We also refuse to ignore the fact that most current religious terrorists are Muslims who justify their actions on religious grounds. In addition, we also fully acknowledge that for centuries Christians slaughtered one another. How they overcame that propensity will be discussed in Chapter 8.

Finally, responses to Muslim terrorism have long generated confessions that terrorism exists because we—Americans, and Westerners in general—have offended Muslims in so many ways, including by supporting Israel, that we really have only ourselves to blame. In the immediate wake of the 9/11 attack, former president Bill Clinton even cited the Crusades as one of "our" crimes against Islam. Rather than dispute that claim here,[11] we merely point out that most Muslim terrorism is against other Muslims. We doubt that even the most ardent apologists for Islam would suppose that either Western or American misdeeds are the reason why Sunni Muslims kill and are killed by Shi'ah.

Chapter Three:
Religious Hostility

Why is the world awash in religious atrocities? What causes people to explode car bombs in one another's neighborhoods or machine-gun worshippers on their way to church? Hating others on the basis of their group membership—their race, nationality, or religion—is one of the oldest sins. And the quest to discover why it occurs probably has generated more social scientific study than any other topic. Unfortunately, no other topic has generated as much flawed theorizing and trivial research. Consequently, we begin this chapter by exposing the defects in the concept of prejudice and move on to explain why it is far more valid to assess intergroup hostilities directly. We then assess data from many nations on religious hostility—measures of anti-Semitism, anti-Christianism, antagonisms between Sunnis and Shi'ah, and anti-Muslimism. Finally, we discuss why religious differences can so easily generate hostility.

Prejudice: A Defective Concept

Any textbook in psychology or sociology will explain that intergroup conflicts are the result of prejudice. And what is prejudice? The standard definition is "the holding of false, negative beliefs about some out-group."[1] These false, negative beliefs (often referred to as stereotypes) are said to cause people to have negative feelings about members of the out-group in question. It is often argued that the "cure" for intergroup hostilities is to educate people as to the falsehood of their prejudices, something that can be facilitated by increased contact with members of the out-group.

The deadly fallacy of this whole line of theorizing is the assumption that the beliefs sustaining the negative feelings are false. Often they aren't! For example, just as most angry Muslims believe, Christians do reject Muhammad's claim to be the successor to Jesus and Moses. And the fact is that Muslims do reject Jesus as the Son of God and do believe that the Qur'an supersedes the Bible. These are only several of the many true beliefs about their religious differences that divide Christians and Muslims. Indeed, it is mostly true beliefs about one another's religion that separate all the major faiths. Thus, any attempt to reduce religious hostilities by revealing them to be based on false, negative beliefs would be absurd, and increased contact might well result in increased hostility. Of course, sometimes the negative beliefs are false—Jews do not control international banking, and the pope is not hiding proof that Jesus married and lived to an old age—but even then it is not clear that increased contact would help matters.

An additional problem with the concept of prejudice is the assumption that the beliefs in question must generate antagonism. But that is far from certain. Many Christians and Muslims, fully aware of the religious disagreements noted above, seem not to let it bother them. Indeed, the elimination of antagonism among religious groups in the United States demonstrates that under certain circumstances, very significant religious differences can be accommodated—as will be considered in Chapter 8. Consequently, here our focus will be directly on hostility, not on prejudice.

Religious Hostility

The best way, and perhaps the only way, to study religious hostility is simply to ask members of various religions how they feel about members of other religions. However, will they answer honestly? Undoubtedly there will be some tendency to minimize negativity, but rather less than one might suppose, because people think their opinions are justified. They don't think they are bigots who must conceal their intolerance because they think their negative feelings are justified. The best evidence that people will admit having negative feelings about others is that, in the data sets analyzed below, so many did so.

Anti-Semitism

Let us begin with the oldest continuing form of religious hostility. The Romans persecuted the Jews long before there were any Christians. But then, for centuries, Western anti-Semitism was rooted in Christian antagonism toward Jews for their rejection of Jesus as the messiah and for their perceived role in the Crucifixion.[2] In the aftermath of World War II and the incredible revelations of the Holocaust, this form of anti-Semitism was pretty much laid to rest—condemned from pulpits all across the Christian denominations. Thus, in 1965, the Second Vatican Council denounced the claim that Jews were responsible for the Crucifixion and condemned anti-Semitism. Since then, several popes have attended services in a synagogue. Elsewhere, interfaith activities have flourished. Today, not only is there little anti-Semitism among Americans, the more religious they are, the less anti-Semitic—Evangelical Protestants being the least anti-Semitic of them all.[3] This development has been bitterly attacked in Muslim publications, and American Muslims are advised to launch a campaign to properly "inform … fundamentalist Protestant ministers."[4]

Unfortunately, as religious anti-Semitism waned among Christians, it became even more malignant among Muslims and some Western leftists, as hatred of Israel and support for Islamic ambitions were transformed into hatred of all Jews wherever they may live.[5] During World War II, some Muslim leaders made common cause with Hitler and the Nazi regime, mainly because of their attacks on Jews. Today, praise for Hitler's treatment of the Jews is noncontroversial in Muslim nations, and exhortations to kill all the Jews are common on Muslim mass media.

- *January 30, 2009*: Egyptian scholar Yusuf al-Qaradawi on the Al-Jazeera Television Network:

  Throughout history, Allah has imposed upon the [Jews], people who would punish them for their corruption. The last punishment was carried out by Hitler. By means of all the things he did to them— even though they exaggerate this issue—he managed to put them in their place. This was divine punishment for them. Allah willing, the next time will be at the hands of the believers.[6]

- *October 16, 2003*: Mahathir bin Mohammad, during his term as prime minister of Malaysia, speaking at a summit meeting of the Organization of the Islamic Conference:

  The Nazis killed six million Jews out of twelve million. But today the Jews rule the world by proxy.

They get others to fight and die for them. They invented socialism, communism, human rights and democracy so that persecuting them would appear to be wrong so they may enjoy equal rights with others. With these they have now gained control of the most powerful countries. And they, this tiny community, have become a world power.[7]

- *January 17, 2009*: Muhammad Hussein Yacoub, Egyptian Islamic scholar, on Al-Raham Television:

You must believe that we will fight, defeat, and annihilate them, until not a single Jew remains on the face of the earth. ... The curse of Allah upon you, whose ancestors were apes and pigs.[8]

Should Saudi Arabian parents ask their children in the eighth grade, "What did you learn in school today?" The kids might quote this from one of their required textbooks:

They are the people of the Sabbath, whose young people God turned into apes, and whose old people God turned into swine to punish them. As cited in Ibn Abbas: The apes are Jews, the keepers of the Sabbath; while the swine are the Christian infidels of the communion of Jesus.[9]

If these Saudi students are in the ninth grade, they will have read this in their textbook: "the annihilation of the Jewish people is imperative."[10]

The results of all this anti-Semitic agitation are on display in Table 3-1 on the following two pages. The data are from the International Social Survey Program, 2008[11], and the Gallup World Polls, 2006-2010.

Relatively speaking, anti-Semitism is low in Europe and in the United States, although higher than one would hope. Elsewhere there is a substantial amount, and overwhelming majorities are anti-Semitic in the Muslim nations—obviously the students in Saudi Arabian schools learned their lessons well, 94 percent of Saudis expressing negative attitudes toward Jews. Notice how Muslim nations stand out in Sub-Saharan Africa—Djibouti (76 percent) and Mauritania (64 percent). Also worth mentioning is that in some European nations, it is local Muslims who swelled their anti-Semitic percentages, and in most

Table 3-1: Anti-Semitism: "What is your personal attitude toward Jews?"

	Percent Negative
Europe	
Belgium	17%
Denmark	10%
Finland	16%
France	9%
Germany	8%
Hungary	14%
Ireland	10%
Latvia	18%
Netherlands	9%
Russia	11%
Slovak Republic	18%
Switzerland	13%
Asia	
Indonesia	50%
Malaysia	52%
Philippines	43%
South Korea	32%
Americas	
Dominican Republic	45%
Uruguay	20%
United States	11%

*Data for the United States are from the Pew Religion and Public Life Survey, 2009.[12]

Table 3-1 (cont.): Anti-Semitism: "What is your personal attitude toward Jews?"

	Percent Negative
Sub-Saharan Africa	
Burkina Faso	20%
Chad	23%
Djibouti	76%
Mali	24%
Mauritania	69%
Niger	59%
Nigeria	31%
Senegal	59%
Sierra Leone	27%
South Africa	24%
Tanzania	30%
North Africa and Middle East	
Algeria	85%
Bangladesh	58%
Iran	48%
Iraq	73%
Lebanon	74%
Pakistan	79%
Palestinian Territories	86%
Saudi Arabia	94%
Syria	78%
Tunisia	86%
Turkey	49%

European nations, persons having no religion were substantially more apt to be anti-Semitic than were the religious (not shown).

Anti-Christianism

Like anti-Semitism, anti-Christianism also began in Rome. Today, antagonism toward Christianity exists among various groups for different reasons. Resentment of Christians, and especially of Christian missionaries, is quite prevalent in India and Asia. As will be seen in Chapter 4, an outbreak of angry atheism has recently developed in Western nations, particularly in the United States, generating remarkably venomous outbursts. But none of this comes close to what is taken for granted by Muslims.

The following quotations are from publications distributed by the Saudi Arabian government and read in mosques around the world. In fact, each of these publications is readily available in most mosques in the United States!

"Be dissociated from the infidels, hate them for their religion … always oppose them in every way according to Islamic law."[13]

"The cursing of Christians is permissible, same as the cursing of the Jews."[14]

"Whoever believes that churches are houses of God and the God is worshipped therein, or that what Jews and Christians do constitutes the worship of God … is an infidel."[15]

"It is forbidden for a Muslim to become citizen of a country [such as the United States] governed by infidels."[16]

So, what about anti-Christianism worldwide? Data are available from the 2008 International Social Survey Program (ISSP),[17] Gallup World Poll (GWP 2006-2010), and the 2008 Pew Research Global Attitudes Survey,[18] all of which asked respondents about their attitudes toward Christians. ISSP and GWP provided responses ranging from positive to negative attitudes, whereas the Pew survey provided favorable versus unfavorable response choices. Table 3.2 presents the results for these questions for respondents who provided an opinion. The responses for the countries included in both the ISSP and GWP and in the Pew surveys suggest that the "negative" response category may be perceived by respondents as more severe than the "unfavorable" response category in the Pew survey, since levels of intolerance in these countries were lower in the ISSP and GWP relative to the Pew survey.

Not surprisingly, Christian European countries have low levels of negative or unfavorable opinions of Christians. Among European countries, France and Spain have the highest percentages of unfavorable attitudes at 17 percent and 26 percent respectively—both probably reflecting anticlerical attitudes based on past political conflicts. Asian countries have considerably higher levels of unfavorable attitudes toward Christians. While India, Japan, and South Korea have similar levels of intolerance (43, 45, and 41 percents respectively), China has the third-highest level of any country (71 percent). (As will be seen, the Chinese are equally intolerant of Muslims).

Levels of Christian intolerance are generally higher in the Americas than in Europe, with 38 percent of Mexicans reporting unfavorable opinions toward Christians. In this region, the United States is set apart, with only 3 percent of the population expressing intolerance toward Christians (most of them being irreligious). Most Sub-Saharan African countries have low levels of Christian intolerance with the exception of Djibouti (64 percent), Mauritania (48 percent), and Niger (37 percent). All three of these countries have Muslim majorities with small Christian populations (less than 2 percent). Other Muslim majority countries in this region with more substantial Christian populations—Burkina Faso (6 percent), Chad (10 percent), and Sierra Leone (5 percent)—have considerably lower levels of Christian intolerance.

The majority of the North African and Middle Eastern countries surveyed have high levels of anti-Christianism. As in Sub-Saharan Africa, the Islamic countries with the highest percentages of negative attitudes—Algeria (57 percent), Bangladesh (47 percent), Pakistan (46 percent), Tunisia (42 percent), Turkey (42 percent), and Saudi Arabia (65 percent)— also have small Christian populations, whereas the countries with lower percentages of negative attitudes— Lebanon (4 percent) and Syria (4 percent)—have larger Christian populations. Iran and Iraq are exceptions, as they both have small Christian populations with relatively lower levels of Christian intolerance, 11 percent and 14 percent respectively.

Table 3.3. "What is your personal attitude toward Christians?"

	ISSP & GWP Percent Negative	Pew Percent Unfavorable
Europe		
Belgium	6%	
Britain	4%	8%
Denmark	2%	
Finland	4%	
France	5%	17%
Germany	3%	13%
Hungary	2%	
Ireland	2%	
Latvia	2%	
Netherlands	4%	
Poland		8%
Russia	1%	8%
Slovak Republic	3%	
Spain		26%
Switzerland	3%	
Asia		
China		71%
India		43%
Indonesia	19%	45%
Japan		45%
South Korea	30%	41%
Americas		
Argentina		18%
Brazil		23%

Table 3.3 (cont.). "What is your personal attitude toward Christians?"

	ISSP & GWP Percent Negative	Pew Percent Unfavorable
Americas (cont.)		
Mexico	11%	38%
United States		3%
Sub-Saharan Africa		
Angola	2%	
Burkina Faso	6%	
Chad	10%	
Djibouti	64%	
Mali	23%	
Mauritania	47%	
Niger	38%	
Nigeria	16%	18%
Sierra Leone	5%	
Senegal	10%	
South Africa	3%	11%
Tanzania	8%	6%
North Africa and Middle East		
Algeria	57%	
Bangladesh	47%	
Egypt		47%
Iran	11%	
Iraq	14%	
Lebanon	4%	15%

Table 3.3 (cont.). "What is your personal attitude toward Christians?"

	ISSP & GWP Percent Negative	Pew Percent Unfavorable
North Africa and Middle East (cont.)		
Pakistan	46%	72%
Saudi Arabia	65%	
Syria	4%	
Tunisia	42%	
Turkey	42%	88%

Sunni vs. Shi'ah

Not all religious hostility is across major religious traditions. In many countries, a substantial proportion of the religious atrocities stem from hostilities between Sunni and Shi'ah Muslims. The Gallup World Poll asked respondents in Islamic countries their attitudes toward Sunnis and Shi'ah. These results are presented in Table 3.3 on the following page.

In most of these nations, Muslims are far more apt to express negative feelings about the Shi'ah than the Sunni. What this reflects, of course, is that nearly all the respondents are themselves Sunni. However, negativity toward the Shi'ah is far lower outside of North Africa and the Middle East—with the exception of Iraq, in which the majority of Muslims are Shi'ah.

The Gallup World Poll also asked respondents in seven Islamic countries whether a basic conflict exists between Sunnis and Shi'ah and whether the relationship between Sunnis and Shi'ah in the world is a concern to the respondent. Table 3.4 presents these results.

Table 3.3 "How do you feel about people of different reli-gious or spiritual groups?" : Muslim Respondents Only

	Feel about *Sunnis* Pecent Negative	Feel about *Shi'ah* Pecent Negative
Algeria	56%	12%
Saudi Arabia	55%	4%
Palestinian Territory	51%	3%
Tunisia	31%	2%
Bangladesh	29%	18%
Pakistan	20%	2%
Turkey	16%	8%
Niger	16%	9%
Senegal	17%	17%
Lebanon	15%	15%
Indonesia	12%	12%
Mauritania	9%	10%
Iraq	8%	10%

A majority of the population in Bangladesh (67 percent), Indonesia (63 percent), and the Palestinian Territories (70 percent) report that a basic conflict exists between Sunnis and Shi'ah. Malaysia and Pakistan have relatively lower percentages of agreement (42 percent and 35 percent respectively), but they also have higher percentages of respondents saying "I don't know"—42 percent in Malaysia and 28 percent in Pakistan. Looking at the percentage of respondents who are concerned about the relationship between Sunnis and Shi'ah, Bangladesh (62 percent) and the Palestinian Territories (54 percent) show the highest levels. Indonesia (16 percent), Malaysia (22 percent), and Pakistan (35 percent) have the lowest levels of agreement but also the highest responses of "I don't know"—75 percent in Indonesia, 62 percent in Malaysia, and 29 percent in Pakistan. In Malaysia, 42 percent of the popula-

Table 3.4: Perceptions of Sunnis and Shi'ah (Muslim Respondents Only*)

	Conflict exists b/w Sunnis & Shi'ah — Percent Yes	Relationship b/w Sunnis & Shi'ah a concern — Percent Yes
Bangladesh	67%	62%
Indonesia	63%	16%
Iran	46%	45%
Malaysia	42%	22%
Pakistan	35%	35%
Palestinian Territories	70%	54%
Turkey	47%	39%

* Respondents who reported "I don't know" remain in the sample.

tion reported not knowing the difference between Sunnis and Shi'ah, as did 34 percent of Indonesian respondents.

Anti-Muslimism

Anti-Muslim feelings arose in Europe soon after the death of Muhammad in response to Islamic invasions of Christian North Africa and, in particular, of southern Italy and most of Spain. Then, in 732 a huge Muslim army based in Spain invaded France, only to be wiped out by a Frankish army at Poitiers after having driven within 150 miles of Paris. These Christian-Muslim conflicts continued during the Crusades and as European forces slowly recovered Italy and Spain. But by the eighteenth century, European fear and antagonism toward Muslims had turned to contempt. Islamic nations were dismissed as backward, and Muslims were regarded as cruel barbarians. Allied forces stationed in North Africa during World War II often referred to local Muslims as "ragheads," in reference to their head scarfs. However, this kind of anti-Muslim expression seems to have died out, even as conflicts based on terrorist attacks have risen. On the other hand, there probably is more negative feeling toward Muslims in Western nations than has been the case for centuries. There were very few for centuries - almost none

The 2008 International Social Survey Program (ISSP)[1] and the 2008 Pew Research Global Attitudes Survey[2] asked respondents about their attitudes toward Muslims. The former provided response choices gauging positive versus negative attitudes, whereas the latter provided favorable versus unfavorable response options. Table 3.5 presents the results for these questions for respondents who provided an opinion.

Table 3.5 "What is your personal attitude toward Muslims?"

	ISSP & GWP Percent Negative	Pew Percent Unfavorable
Europe		
Belgium	36%	
Britain		26%
Denmark	36%	
Finland	64%	
France	26%	38%
Germany		55%
Hungary	20%	
Ireland	19%	
Latvia	31%	
Netherlands	32%	
Poland		57%
Russia	9%	37%
Slovak Republic	40%	
Spain		61%
Switzerland	23%	
Asia		
China		73%
India		61%
Indonesia		2%

Table 3.5 (cont.)"What is your personal attitude toward Muslims?"

	ISSP & GWP Percent Negative	Pew Percent Unfavorable
Asia (cont.)		
Japan		74%
South Korea	34%	63%
Americas		
Argentina		74%
Brazil		29%
Mexico		74%
United States		29%
Sub-Saharan Africa		
Nigeria		21%
Tanzania		14%
South Africa	22%	58%
North Africa and Middle East		
Egypt		1%
Jordan		1%
Lebanon		4%
Pakistan		1%
Turkey	2%	10%

Looking at the ISSP results, in nearly all of the countries, a minority of respondents expressed negative attitudes toward Muslims. Finland (64 percent) and the Slovak Republic (40 percent) have the highest percentages of negative attitudes toward Muslims. On the other hand, the Pew results show that in eleven countries the majority of respondents indicated unfavorable attitudes toward Muslims.

In Europe there is considerable across-country variability in unfavorable attitudes toward Muslims, with the majority of respondents in Germany, Poland, and Spain reporting unfavorable attitudes, and a minority of respondents in Britain, France, and Russia reporting the same. There is considerably less across-country variability in Asia and the Americas, where in all the countries surveyed except the United States, over 60 percent of their respondents expressed unfavorable attitudes toward Muslims—except, of course for Muslim Indonesia. As would be expected, in Islamic countries, very few respondents expressed unfavorable attitudes toward Muslims.

Table 3.6 compares the responses of Christians and those with no religion in countries in which there are sufficient numbers of both. In most of these countries, Christians and those with no religious affiliation have similar attitudes toward Muslims, and thus most of the variation in tolerance is across countries. Argentina stands out, with Christians (65 percent) being substantially more likely than those with no religion (45 percent) to acknowledge negative attitudes toward Muslims. An opposite contrast occurs in Latvia, where 25 percent of the Christians versus 39 percent of those with no religion expressed negative attitudes.

Interestingly, in Indonesia, Lebanon, and Pakistan, the percentages reported for unfavorable attitudes toward Muslims are smaller than the percentages reported for negative attitudes toward Sunnis and Shiites. In Indonesia, 2 percent of respondents reported unfavorable attitudes toward Muslims versus 12 percent for Sunnis and Shiites. Similarly, while 12 percent of respondents in Lebanon expressed negative attitudes toward Sunnis and Shiites, only 4 percent expressed unfavorable opinions toward Muslims. What this reflects is that the unfavorable attitudes toward Muslims mostly are expressed by each nation's tiny Christian population, while hostility toward Sunnis and Shi'ah reflect disputes within the large Muslim populations. Thus, in Pakistan, where Sunnis outnumber Shi'ah by four to one, 2 percent of the population expressed negative attitudes toward Sunnis, whereas 20 percent expressed negative attitudes toward Shi'ah.

The 2009 Pew Survey on Religion and Public Life,[21] a survey of Americans, asked more specific questions regarding attitudes toward Muslims. Respondents were given two

Table 3.6 "What is your personal attitude toward Muslims?"

	ISSP Percent Negative		Pew Percent Unfavorable	
	Christian	No Religion	Christian	No Religion
Europe				
Belgium	35%	41%		
Britain			24%	30%
Denmark	37%	30%		
Finland	65%	58%		
France	26%	27%	39%	39%
Germany			58%	61%
Hungary	21%	15%		
Ireland	19%	19%		
Latvia	25%	39%		
Netherlands	32%	33%		
Russia	8%	16%	38%	49%
Slovak Republic	40%	37%		
Spain			64%	61%
Switzerland	23%	26%		
Asia				
South Korea			71%	62%
Amerias				
Argentina			65%	45%
Brazil			63%	63%

statements and asked which came closest to their own views: (1) The Islamic religion is more likely than others to encourage violence among its believers, or (2) The Islamic religion does not encourage violence more than others. Of those who chose a statement, 45 percent picked statement one, consistent with the fact that 43 percent of the sample also expressed unfavorable opinions toward Muslims. And yet 46 percent of respondents identified knowing someone who was Muslim. In fact, 42 percent of those who believed Islamic religion encourages violence said they knew a Muslim. So much, then, for the notion that contact with Muslims will decrease negative beliefs. Not surprisingly, a majority of American respondents (67 percent) identified Muslims as experiencing a lot of discrimination. But what do American Muslims themselves report?

In a 2007 survey of American Muslims conducted by the Pew Research Center[22], 26 percent reported that they have been a victim of discrimination as a Muslim living in the United States. Reflecting on experiences they had in the past twelve months, 26 percent of the sample said that people had acted suspicious of them, 15 percent reported being called offensive names, 18 percent claimed to have been singled out by airport security, and 4 percent stated that they had been physically threatened or attacked.

To sum up: there is a great deal of religious hostility around the globe. An overwhelming majority of the world's Muslims admit to anti-Semitism. There are high levels of Anti-Christianism in Asian and Muslim nations, and the Shi'ah are hated in Sunni nations. Finally, there is a substantial amount of negative feeling toward Muslims in the non-Muslim nations.

Religious Particularism

It is time to explore why religious hostility is so widespread. In the first major sociological study ever conducted of religious hostility, the concept of religious particularism was introduced and defined as "commitment to a doctrine of exclusive religious truth; the belief that there is only one true faith."[23] Particularism is inherent in the conceptions of God sustained by the great monotheisms: Judaism, Christianity, and Islam. Each asserts that there is but one God, and that to believe otherwise is a grievous sin.

Although each of these faiths believes there is but one true God, none has been unable to sustain one true faith. Rather, from the beginning, each of the three major monotheisms has been prone to splinter into many "true" religions. Ancient Israel was wracked with conflicts—the Talmud noted the existence of twenty-four disputatious factions.[24] Thus, Pharisees denounced the Sadducees, and the Essenes condemned them both, while zealots known as the Sicarii lurked in public places to stab prominent Jews, including High Priests, whom they deemed insufficiently pious. So, too, did early Christians devote much energy to denouncing one another—among the earliest Christian documents are *catalogs of heresy*! In about the year 180, Irenaeus produced his famous five-volume attack on heresy, wherein he listed nearly two dozen groups of Christians who had strayed from the True Faith. A few years later Hippolytus issued an expanded catalog listing nearly fifty heretical groups.[25] And so it continued, resulting in centuries of massacres and holy wars. In similar fashion, from the earliest times, Islam has always been plagued by bitter and often violent sectarianism. The original schism into Sunni and Shi'ah Muslims was reported in Chapter 2. But there are dozens of other Muslim groups—there even are many divisions within both the Sunni and the Shi'ah—and each and every one of them regards all the others as sinfully wrong.

Of course, there was even far more diversity of doctrines and practices within classical paganism. But in the absence of claims to exclusive truth, these pagan differences produced no sparks. The priests of various temples undoubtedly regarded one another as competitors for patronage, and it seems likely that sometimes priests of one temple were a bit contemptuous of those serving another, but this was far more like the feelings a modern auto dealer has for another dealer down the street. As a perceptive pagan told St. Augustine (*Epistle* 16), the temples existed in a state of "concordant discord."

In contrast, particularistic religions always contain the potential for dangerous conflicts because *theological disagreements seem inevitable:* heresy is inherent in the act of seeking to fully understand the meaning of scripture, for humans inevitably reach differing conclusions. Heresy also will continue to arise because of the frequency with which deeply religious people have what they perceive to be revelations. Of course, many of these will merely confirm the prevailing religion, but some will be innovative.[26] Therefore, the decisive factor governing religious hatred and conflict is whether, and to what degree, religious disagreement—pluralism, if you will—is tolerated.

It must be recognized that nonparticularistic religions are not always tolerant, especially not of particularistic competitors. In Roman times, pagans actively persecuted both Jews and Christians, and today, both Hindus and Buddhists have been known to assert that theirs are the true faiths in response to Christians and Muslims. Indeed, both Hindus and Buddhists have committed violent acts of persecution against Muslims and Christians, as well as against one another.

Chapter 8 examines how toleration of religious disagreement was achieved in the highly pluralistic American religious culture. Here it seems appropriate to examine the degree to which unmitigated particularism persists in the United States, in contrast with Muslim nations.

Table 3-7 is based on two Baylor National Religion Surveys conducted by the Gallup Poll.

Table 3-7: Particularism Among Americans

"My religion is the one, true faith that leads to salvation"			
Percent agree	21%		
"How many of the following people do you think will get into heaven?"			
Christians			
Percent "none"	0%	Percent "a few"	6%
Muslims			
Percent "none"	15%	Percent "a few"	11%
Buddhists			
Percent "none"	16%	Percent "a few"	8%
Jews			
Percent "none"	5%	Percent "a few"	11%
Non-Religious People			
Percent "none"	21%	Percent "a few"	13%

Only one out of five Americans believes that theirs is the one true faith with an exclusive claim on salvation. Consequently, most Americans regard the Gates of Heaven as wide open. Only 21 percent think that even nonreligious people won't get in, while 13 percent expect that they will be limited to only "a few." Not many (15 percent) think all Muslims are excluded, 16 percent put Buddhists in the same situation, and only 5 percent think Jews can't get in. That Americans are so unwilling to exclude other religions, and even nonbelievers, from salvation probably reflects popularization of the innovative Catholic doctrine of the "unconscious Catholic."

For many years, the great stumbling block to amicable relations between American Catholics and Protestants was the Catholic doctrine *extra ecclesiam nulla salus*—that there is no salvation outside the Church, thus consigning Protestants, Jews, and everyone else to hell. Then, agonizing over what he was being told about Nazi death camps, in June 1943 Pope Pius XII issued an encyclical that opened the door for reconciliation of all the faiths. In *Mystici Corpus Christi* (On the Mystical Body of Christ), the pope wrote that God's mercy would extend to all persons of *implicit faith*—persons with a sincere desire for genuine faith—for this qualified them as Catholics although they were unaware of it. In November 1964, this doctrine was extended by the Vatican II Council as it acknowledged that many elements of religious truth "can exist outside the visible boundaries of the Catholic church."[27] These views were echoed by all of the major American Protestant denominations, thus enabling sincere Christians to have things both ways: Christianity is the one true religion, but sincere believers in other religions are thereby among God's own.

Not so, or at least not yet so, among the world's Muslims. Early in 2013, the Pew Forum released a major set of surveys conducted of Muslims in a number of nations.[28] Table 3-8 shows some of the results as to particularism.

Table 3-8: Particularism Among Muslims

"Islam is the one true faith leading to eternal life in heaven."	
	Percent of Muslims Who Agree
Egypt	96%
Jordan	96%
Iraq	95%
Morocco	94%
Malaysia	93%
Pakistan	92%
Palestinian Terr.	89%
Bangladesh	88%
Indonesia	87%
Turkey	74%
Tunisia	72%
Lebanon	66%
United States	44%[29]

In these nations where nearly everyone is a Muslim, particularism is nearly universal. But among Muslims in the United States, the majority no longer claim that only Muslims will enter heaven, albeit a very large minority (44 percent) still hold that position.

In subsequent chapters, as we confront evidence of Muslim support for terrorism, keep in mind that part of their motivation may be to keep people from going to hell by imposing Muslim religion upon them. Indeed, overwhelming majorities in these same Muslim nations also believe it is their religious duty to convert others.[30] Unfortunately, they also believe that any Muslim who converts to another religion should be beheaded.

This is an excuse for killing people.

Chapter Four:
Conflicts of Irreligion

Although the primary focus of our study is on the hostilities that religious groups harbor toward one another, irreligious people are hardly immune. As will be seen, there is an abundance of irreligious hostility toward the religious, who tend to respond in kind.

Angry Atheists

Western civilization had long harbored angry atheists determined to put an end to religion. Voltaire (1694-1778) loathed religion and believed it would disappear within the next fifty years. His friend Denis Diderot (1713-1984) hoped for "the last of the kings to be strangled by the guts of the last priest." During the nineteenth century, a very popular public orator, Robert Ingersol (1833-1899), regaled American audiences with very humorous attacks on the Bible, and some of the most influential European philosophers, including Auguste Comte (1798-1857) and Friedrich Nietzsche (1844-1900) were militant atheists. Slowly, irreligiousness filtered into the European and American universities, particularly into the leading divinity schools. In fact, the first militant Darwinian hired at Harvard did not join the faculty of the biology department but of the Harvard Divinity School, where, upon his arrival, Crawford Howell Toy (1836-1919) announced that he wished "to be known as a Theist rather than a Christian."[1] Subsequently, the elite divinity schools became strongholds for Paul Tillich's (1886-1965) "theology," which conceives of God as entirely symbolic.

Eventually atheism became dominant in the social science departments, as well. Thus, according to the distinguished American anthropologist Anthony F.C. Wallace, in his very popular undergraduate textbook, *Religion: An Anthropological View*, "the evolutionary future of religion is extinction. Belief in supernatural beings and in supernatural forces that affect nature without obeying nature's laws will erode and become only an interesting memory ... belief in supernatural powers is doomed to die out, all over the world, as a result of the increasing adequacy and diffusion of scientific knowledge ... the process is inevitable."[2]

At about the same time, the well-known sociologist Peter Berger told the *New York Times* that by "the 21st century, religious believers are likely to be found only in small sects, huddled together to resist a worldwide secular culture ... the predicament of the believer is increasingly like that of a Tibetan astrologer on a prolonged visit to an American university."[3] In light of the recent lionization of the Dalai Lama by the American media and his cordial welcome on many campuses, Berger's simile now admits to an ironic interpretation. And, in fact, in 1997 Berger gracefully took it all back, noting that if anything, the world had gotten more religious during the interim.

But, most of Berger's colleagues remain antagonistic to religion. A national survey of members of the American Association for the Advancement of Science, conducted in 2009 by the Pew Research Center, found that only 33 percent said they believed in God, 18 percent did not believe in God but believed in a universal spirit or higher power, and 41 percent believed in neither (7 percent refused to answer). Remarkably, a study conducted in 1914 found almost identical results.

In any event, in the past several years an explosion of popular books by angry and remarkably nasty atheists have hit the bestseller list:

- *The God Delusion* by Richard Dawkins (2006)

- *Breaking the Spell* by Daniel C. Dennett (2006)

- *God is Not Great: How Religion Poisons Everything* by Christopher Hitchens (2007)

As for nasty: Dawkins charged that teaching children about religion ought to be recognized as "child abuse" and outlawed. Dennett refers to atheists as "brights" in contrast with those dullards who still cling to faith. And all three authors propose that just about every brutal moment in history was caused by religion remarkably they avoid acknowledging that the twentieth century was the bloodiest in history because of staunchly antireligious tyrants: Hitler, Stalin, and Mao.

Pol Pot

Since these books sold well, it was widely assumed that they signaled a breakthrough for atheism, that large numbers of Americans were now ready to stand up and admit they didn't believe in God. That seemed to be confirmed by claims that the number of Americans who say they have no religious affiliation had climbed sharply in recent years[4] (the Baylor surveys placed their number at 11 percent). But this "evidence" soon crumbled because those making this claim were so careless that they hadn't bothered to check on the actual religiousness of those who report having no religion. It turns out that the majority of them pray, and the great majority are not atheists![5] Apparently, what most people who say they have no religion mean is not that they are irreligious, but that they have no church.

So, what about atheists? Is their number growing? Recall that atheism has not grown among scientists in nearly a century, and Table 4-1 shows that the percentage of atheists in the general population hasn't increased at all, either!

Table 4-1: Year and Percent of Americans Who Do Not Believe in God

1944 (Gallup)	4%
1947 (Gallup)	6%
1964 (American Piety)	3%
1994 (GSS)	3%
2005 (Baylor Survey)	4%
2007 (Baylor Survey)	4%

One reason the percentage of atheists has not grown is that irreligion is not effectively transmitted from parents to children. Studies show that the majority of children born into a home having no religion end up joining a religious group—most often a conservative denomination.[6]

Nor is it only in the United States that atheists are scarce and where their numbers are not growing. Despite the fact that Americans are far more religious than people in most other advanced industrial nations, atheism has failed to take hold in these other nations, as well, as is shown in Table 4-2.

Table 4-2: Atheism in the Industrialized Nations (cont.)

Percent "I am a convinced atheist."	
Canada	4%
New Zealand	5%
Australia	5%
Western Europe	
Austria	2%
Ireland	2%
Italy	3%
Iceland	3%
Finland	3%
Portugal	3%
Switzerland	4%
Norway	4%
Greece	4%
Denmark	5%
Great Britain	5%
Netherlands	6%
Sweden	6%
Spain	6%
Germany	7%
Belgium	7%
France	14%

An immense amount has been written about irreligious and secularized Europeans. But atheists they are not. Even in France, famous for its anticlerical and antireligious politics, only 14 percent say they do not believe in God. As for "Godless" Finland and Iceland, 3 percent say they are atheists, precisely the same as in "priest-ridden" Italy.

By far the most interesting data in this table are those for the former Soviet Bloc. For more than seventy years, atheists controlled the Soviet state and enforced an official policy of atheism. Beginning in the first year of school, and each year all the way through college, students in the Soviet Union were required to take a course in atheism. Following World War II,

Table 4-2: Atheism in the Industrialized Nations (cont.)

Former Soviet Bloc	
Poland	1%
Romania	1%
Georgia	1%
Ukraine	3%
Latvia	3%
Russia	4%
Slovakia	4%
Hungary	5%
Albania	5%
Bulgaria	6%
Czech Republic	8%
Asia	
Taiwan	2%
India	4%
Japan	12%

Source: World Values Surveys, 1999-2002

when the Soviets took control of the nations of Eastern Europe, a similar system of atheist education was imposed. Year after year, students were rehearsed in all the angry antireligious arguments to be found in recent tracts such as Richard Dawkins' *The God Delusion*. And it wasn't merely education that atheism had going for it in the Soviet Bloc. There was intense discrimination against religious people"if you wanted to have a good job, you professed atheism. If you were too intensely or too overtly religious, you might get sent to a hard labor camp or even be killed. The result? In Russia itself the score is: God, 96 percent, atheism, 4 percent, precisely the same as in the United States. Nor did the atheism campaign do significantly better anywhere in the rest of the old Soviet Bloc.

In his wonderful recent book, *The Plot to Kill God: Findings From the Soviet Experiment in Secularization*,[7] Paul Froese demonstrates the utter ineptitude of the Soviet efforts to instill atheism. In part, the educational program made no progress because it was staffed by, and the teaching materials were prepared by, people who knew next to nothing about religion. The assumption was that since religion is nonsense, there is nothing much one needs to know to refute it. Hence, what the atheism faculty regarded as unanswerable criticisms of faith were, in fact, quite elementary matters of theology and easily refuted by the average church-goer.

The ineptitudes of Soviet attacks on religion also dominate the current crop of books on atheism. To expect to learn anything about important theological problems from Richard Dawkins or Daniel Dennett is like expecting to learn about medieval history from someone who had only read *Robin Hood*. This criticism has been expressed by many reviewers, even by those who are themselves atheists! Thus, the biologist H. Allen Orr, writing in *The New York Review of Books*, noted that he had once called Richard Dawkins a "professional atheist," but "I'm forced after reading his book [*The God Delusion*] to conclude that he's actually more of an amateur."[8] And, writing in *The London Review of Books*, the Marxist literary scholar Terry Eagleton dismissed Dawkins' characterization of religious beliefs as such silliness that "not even the dim-witted clerics who knocked me about in grammar school thought like that."[9]

So why have books by angry atheists been selling well? For one thing, 4 percent of the population of more than 300 million Americans amounts to more than 12 million people"a lot of them potential book buyers. For another thing, this 4 percent is greatly overrepresented in the media, especially among book reviewers, and so the books receive maximum coverage. But perhaps most of all, as Michael Novak suggested in a very perceptive article, both the authors and their readers may be animated, not by confidence that their time has come, but by despair. As Novak put it, "there is an odd defensiveness about all these books"as though they were a sign not of victory but of desperation."[10]

Novak's perceptions are confirmed by a very recent study based on interviews with people prominent in atheist organizations. Many expressed sentiments consistent with the idea that it is frustration for the lack of growth that has produced these angry outbursts"that American atheists have come to feel like embattled members of a very unfashionable, unpopular religious sect.[11] Fully in keeping with this conclusion, compared with other people, atheists are not comfortable talking about religion with their neighbors or co-workers. In fact, they tend to be uncomfortable talking about religion even with their friends and their families![12]

Anti-Evangelicalism

A survey of a national sample of college and university professors conducted in 2006 found that 53 percent admitted to having negative feelings toward Evangelical Protestants, compared with 3 percent having such feelings toward Jews and 18 percent toward atheists.[13] In 2009, the Pew Forum surveyed a national sample of Americans and found that while only 3 percent said they had an unfavorable attitude toward Christians, 24 percent had an unfavorable attitude toward Evangelical Christians.[14] Of course, irreligious Americans were even more inclined this way, 46 percent giving a negative rating to Evangelicals, just as it was the irreligious academics who most disliked Evangelicals. It seems likely that these negative attitudes were partly due to a raft of recent books warning about Evangelical conspiracies.

In his best-selling *American Theocracy* (2007), Kevin Phillips identified former president George Bush as the "Theocrat-in-Chief," described Evangelicals as the victims of "half-baked preaching," and peppered his book with quotations denouncing Evangelicals, such as Harvey Cox's claim that evangelical religion is a "toxin endangering the health—even the life—of the Christian churches and American society."[15] This earned Phillips fulsome praise in *Time* magazine, *The New York Times*, and other major media outlets. Even so, Phillips was topped by the atheist Sam Harris, who claimed that "Tens of millions of our neighbors are working each day to obliterate the separation of church and state, to supplant scientific rationality with Iron Age fantasies, and to achieve a Christian theocracy in the twenty-first century."[16] Most recently, in *The Child Catchers* (2013) Kathryn Joyce charges that Evangelicals are eagerly involved in a worldwide plot to adopt children from non-Western societies and raise them as Christians in order to undermine all other faiths!

So many books warning against evil Evangelicals have been published that they nearly constitute a separate literary genre—although the number of new titles has been declining in the past several years. Unfortunately, even most of the more temperate and informed commentators on the politics of Evangelical Americans share with the atheists the belief that Evangelicals are very different from other Americans, that they are far more conservative on all cultural issues and that they are extremists in their opposition to the separation of church and state.

Given how often questions about these matters are included in national surveys, it is amazing that little or no effort has been devoted to documenting these charges against Evangelicals. Perhaps they are regarded as so self-evident as to need no factual substantiation. Or could it be because the facts are quite otherwise?

Typically, Evangelical respondents to surveys have been identified on the basis of their denominational affiliation. Hence, Baptists, Nazarenes, Pentecostals, and members of other "conservative" denominations are classified as Evangelicals, while Presbyterians, Episcopalians, and other religious "liberals" are excluded. This is very unsatisfactory for two reasons. First, when given the opportunity to identify themselves as Evangelicals in the 2007 Baylor National Religion Survey, many members of conservative denominations did not do so. Second, many members of the more liberal denominations, and even some Roman Catholics, did claim to be Evangelicals. This can be observed in Table 4-3.

Obviously, to infer who is and is not an Evangelical from their denominational affiliation is, at best, a very inaccurate

Table 4-3: Who Is an Evangelical?

	Identified Themselves as Evangelicals
Conservative Protestants	49%
NonDenominational Protestants	44%
Liberal Protestants	28%
Roman Catholics	14%
No Religion	2%
Total Sample	28%

Source: Baylor National Religious Survey, 2007

measure and justified only (if ever) when self-identification data are unavailable. Moreover, this is why the proper term is Evangelical Christian, not Evangelical Protestant.

Recall from the Introduction that a major conflict has been going on in the United States over public religious expression, on major matters of school prayers and the display of religious symbols in public places. Evangelical Christians are widely accused of wishing to reverse these rulings, and this is frequently offered as evidence of their theocratic aims. These claims are tested in Table 4-4.

If one looked only at the third section of this table, one might agree that Evangelicals pose a threat to the strict separation of church and state—only a third support it. But that interpretation must change dramatically when one looks at the upper two parts of the table. There we see that while most Evangelicals do agree that it ought to be legal to display religious symbols in public places, so does most everyone else. The same is true of school prayer. What seems evident is that Evangelicals are better informed as to what "strict" separation of church and state means—that it prohibits school prayers and public religious displays, among other things. For most Americans, their support for strict separation of church and state would seem to be merely a slogan that has the blessing of the media, and they are unaware that it is in contradiction to their specific views. The most important lesson to be drawn from these three items in Table 4-4 is that if a national referendum were held to restore school prayer and to allow such things as nativity scenes on public property, even if Evangelicals were not allowed to vote, the referendum would pass by a landslide.

Items 4 and 5 also show that the Evangelicals aren't that different from other Americans on these leading cultural issues, either. While only 16 percent of Evangelicals would repeal the death penalty, only 20 percent of non-Evangelicals would do so. It is true that Evangelicals are nearly unanimous in their opposition to abortion on these grounds, but nearly two-thirds of non-Evangelicals agree with them.

Back in the 1940s and 1950s, there were many popular books and articles in magazines such as *The Nation* that exposed the secret plans by the Pope and his Catholic minions to take over America and stamp out all traces of democracy. In

Table 4-4: Are Evangelicals Different?

"Do you agree or disagree that the federal government should:

1. *allow the display of religious symbols in public spaces?*   **Agree**

Evangelicals	88%
Liberal Protestants	72%
Roman Catholics	74%
No Religion	26%
All Non-Evangelicals	61%

2. *allow prayer in public schools?*   **Agree**

Evangelicals	94%
Liberal Protestants	67%
Roman Catholics	76%
No Religion	21%
All Non-Evangelicals	60%

3. *enforce a strict separation of church and state?*   **Agree**

Evangelicals	33%
Liberal Protestants	53%
Roman Catholics	54%
No Religion	81%
All Non-Evangelicals	58%

4. *abolish the death penalty?*   **Agree**

Evangelicals	16%
Liberal Protestants	20%
Roman Catholics	18%
No Religion	34%
All Non-Evangelicals	20%

5. *Abortion is wrong when the only reason is that the woman does not want the child.*   **Agree**

Evangelicals	94%
Liberal Protestants	60%
Roman Catholics	75%
No Religion	24%
All Non-Evangelicals	63%

Source: Baylor National Religion Survey 2007.

his 1949 best seller, *American Freedom and Catholic Power*, Paul Blanshard devoted many pages to details of the theocratic regime the Pope had in store for America, if he were not headed off. Blanshard proposed that Protestant Americans organize "a resistance movement to prevent the [Catholic] hierarchy from imposing its social policies upon our schools, hospitals, government and family organizations."[17]

Today, these anti-Catholic concerns seem ridiculous. Hopefully, the equally spurious claims about Evangelical theocratic plots will also soon seem ridiculous, as well. For the fact is that Evangelicals are not very different after all.

Anti-Atheism

Not only is there no research literature on anti-Atheism, the term is not even included in the immense literature on prejudice, religious or otherwise—although one writer in the journal *Religious Humanism* has proposed the unattractive term Atheophobia.[18] Therefore, we were extremely surprised to discover that both the Gallup World Poll and the International Social Survey Program[19] have asked about attitudes toward atheists in many nations. The combined results appear in Table 4-5 on the following page.

Europeans are very tolerant of atheists—in many nations fewer than 10 percent express negative views, and even in Finland, only 29 percent do so. In contrast, people in Muslim nations are almost unanimous in saying they have a negative view of atheists. This should be no surprise, since atheism is effectively against the law in many of these nations. In fact, anyone born a Muslim who then professes atheism is regarded as an apostate and is to be punished by death. We explore popular support for executing apostates in Chapter 5.

But if antagonism toward atheists is highest in the Muslim nations, it also is quite high in Sub-Saharan Africa, where about two-thirds take a dim view of atheists. This is consistent with the fact that in several nations where there are a sufficient number of both Christian and Muslim respondents to make comparisons, there is little difference between them in their dislike of atheists, as can be seen in Table 4-6.

The precarious situation of Christians in most of these nations has not made them more sympathetic toward atheists.

Table 4-5: "What is your personal attitude toward atheists or nonbelievers?

	Percent Negative
Europe	
Belgium	13%
Denmark	7%
Finland	29%
France	5%
Germany	14%
Hungary	13%
Ireland	18%
Latvia	9%
Netherlands	9%
Russia	6%
Slovak Republic	15%
Switzerland	8%
United Kingdom	13%
Islamic Nations	
Algeria	81%
Bangladesh	75%
Indonesia	76%
Iraq	83%
Lebanon	87%
Mauritania	87%
Niger	79%
Pakistan	88%
Palestinian Territories	92%
Saudi Arabia	95%
Senegal	86%
Tunisia	94%
Turkey	68%
Sub-Saharan Africa	
Angola	68%
Nigeria	65%
South Africa	41%
Tanzania	69%

Table 4-6: Comparing Christians and Muslims in their Attitudes Toward Atheists

Nation	Percent having negative feelings toward atheists	
	Christians	Muslims
Lebanon	83%	90%
Pakistan	64%	89%
Indonesia	71%	78%
Nigeria	64%	67%
Senegal	83%	86%
South Africa	43%	42%

Six times, beginning in 2001 and ending in 2009, the Pew Research Center has asked a national sample of Americans whether they had a favorable or unfavorable opinion "of Atheists, this is, people who don't believe in God."[20] Each time about a third said they had a favorable opinion of atheists, and about two-thirds said they had an unfavorable opinion.

Clearly, the tendency for atheists to feel embattled, noted earlier in the chapter, seems justified. They are rather unpopular, if not in Europe, then elsewhere.

Chapter Five: Embracing Religious Extremism

It is one thing to think that yours is the only true religion. It is quite something else to be willing to kill people who reject your religion or to murder former members of your religion who have converted to another faith. Unfortunately, there are many people who are eager to impose the death penalty on "unbelievers," "heretics," "apostates," "adulterers," and other such malefactors. And in addition to all these lethal extremists are millions who condone their actions. The latter are the focus of this chapter. Because Muslims so dominate the ranks of religious terrorists and most of these actions occur in Muslim nations, our focus necessarily will be on the Islamic world.

Hurra for Jihad

The events of September 11[h], 2001, when Muslim suicidal terrorists flew two airplanes into the World Trade Center and one into the side of the Pentagon, were denounced around the world. But what does the Muslim public really think about this event?

First of all, overwhelming majorities do not believe that a group of Arabs flew the planes! A Pew Research Survey of seven Islamic nations conducted in 2011 found that only 28 percent of Lebanese Muslims believed that Arabs did it, and belief was lower elsewhere—only 9 percent of Turks believed it. Presumably most Muslims agree with the so-called American "Truthers," who think that George W. Bush staged the whole thing.

In any event, the Gallup World Poll asked respondents to what extent the events of September 11th in the United States can be morally justified. Overall, 22 percent of the world's Muslims responded that these events were justified.[1] But opinion varies considerably by country, as can be seen in Table 5.1, which shows the percentage of Muslims in each country who reported that the events of 9/11 were justified.

Table 5.1. Were the Events of September 11, 2001 in the United States Justified?

Percent of Muslims who thought 9/11 was justified	
Djibouti	48%
Palestinian Territories	43%
Guinea	43%
Chad	31%
Yemen	30%
Mali	29%
Sudan	27%
Bahrain	27%
Egypt	26%
Pakistan	26%
Jordan	25%
Senegal	25%
Comoros	25%
Afghanistan	24%
Algeria	23%
Mauritania	23%
Niger	23%
Sierra Leone	22%
Iraq	22%
Syria	22%
Tunisia	21%
Lebanon	21%
Saudi Arabia	21%
Ethiopia	20%
Malaysia	18%
Bangladesh	16%
Kuwait	13%
Turkey	12%
Iran	10%
Great Britain	7%
France	6%

In all the countries surveyed, only a minority of Muslims felt that the events of September 11th were justified—but, of course, the large majority in each nation who thinks the whole thing was staged by Americans is unlikely to think it justified. Whatever the case, in several countries a very substantial minority agreed it was justified: Djibouti (48 percent), the Palestinian Territories (43 percent), and Guinea (43 percent). In most of the Islamic nations in Africa and the Middle East, 20 to 30 percent of Muslims believe that the events of September 11th were justified. Obviously, the opinions of Muslims in Europe—Great Britain and France—have been influenced by the prevailing climate of opinion on the media to which they are exposed. Yet some may see dangerous signs for possible domestic terrorism in the fact that even 6 or 7 percent supported this suicide attack.

But what about suicide bombings more generally? The Pew Forum on Religion and Public Life asked Muslims in various countries whether suicide bombing and other forms of vio-

Table 5.2. Is Suicide Bombing in Defense of Islam Justified?[2]

Percent of Muslims Who Responded Sometimes or Often Justified	
Palestinian Territories	40%
Afghanistan	39%
Egypt	29%
Bangladesh	26%
Malaysia	18%
Turkey	15%
Jordan	15%
Pakistan	13%
Tunisia	12%
Morocco	9%
United States*	8%
Iraq	7%

* From the 2007 and 2011 Pew Surveys of U.S. Muslims (percentage remained constant across years).

lence against civilian targets are justified in order to defend Islam from its enemies. Table 5.2 shows the percentage of Muslims in each country who condoned such terrorist tactics. Percentages are depressed because Pew did not remove nonrespondents from the calculations. Those without an opinion, who responded "don't know," also are included in the base.

Consistent with opinions about September 11th, in each of these countries only a minority of Muslims believe that suicide bombings are often or sometimes justified, but again these are large minorities in the Palestinian Territories (40 percent), Afghanistan (39 percent) and Egypt (29 percent). Note, too, that Muslims in Iraq are least supportive. We suggest that what this reflects is that most Muslims in Iraq feel personally at risk from this form of terrorism—as well they should, given the frequency of such incidents and the very high death rate that prevails. Note that 8 percent of American Muslims support suicide bombing, which is similar to support for 9/11 among Muslims in Great Britain and France. One supposes that this group of Americans would have included the Tsarnaev brothers, had they been included in the sample.

Deadly Conversion

- *Egypt.* January 10, 2013: A criminal court sentenced Nadia Mohamed Ali and her seven children to fifteen years in prison each for having converted from Islam to Christianity.

Nadia and her children were lucky—in Egypt "apostates" can be sentenced to death. In some nations, including Afghanistan and Saudi Arabia, death is the *mandatory* sentence for quitting Islam. The Pew Forum on Religion and Public Life has published surveys in which Muslims were asked whether they favor or oppose the death penalty for people who leave the Muslim religion.[3] Table 5.3 presents their findings.

Support for killing defectors from the faith is depressingly high in most of these nations. In Egypt, 88 percent would have given their approval had Nadia and her children been executed! Jordanians (83 percent) are nearly as favorable. Only in Tunisia (18 percent), Lebanon (17 percent) and Turkey (8 percent) is there little support, and these are three of the most "secular" Muslim nations.

Table 5.3. Death Penalty for People who Leave the Muslim Religion?

Percent of Muslims who Favor the Death Penalty for Apostasy	
Egypt	88%
Jordan	83%
Afghanistan	79%
Pakistan	75%
Palestinian Territories	62%
Djibouti	62%
Malaysia	58%
Bangladesh	43%
Iraq	41%
Tunisia	18%
Lebanon	17%
Turkey	8%

Honor Killings

Too often, families kill a wife or daughter (and rarely a son) because they believe they have dishonored the family, usually being suspected of sexual misdeeds. Many of the cases are truly bizarre: a young girl strangled by her family for having been raped by her cousins. A girl killed by her brother when he discovered she owned a cell phone—he assumed she must have been using it for immoral purposes. A young woman beaten to death by her brothers for wearing slacks. Or the couple who eloped without the permission of the girl's family and who were hanged from a tree while the neighbors laughed.

Each of these incidents occurred during 2012 and was included in our Atrocities Index. In all, we identified seventy-eight honor killings, forty-five of them in Pakistan. Obviously these are but a small fraction of the honor killings that occurred, since we could only learn of those reported in the world press, and many (perhaps most) occur in villages and are never even reported to local officials.

The Pew Forum on Religion and Public Life's (2013) report on global religious restrictions also identified sixty-five countries (33 percent of their sample) in which "individuals or groups used violence or the threat of violence, including so-called honor killings, to try to enforce religious norms."[4] Although Hindus and Sikhs commit honor killings, most are perpetrated by Muslims.[5] Many Muslim advocacy groups argue that domestic violence is present in all religious traditions, not just Islam, and that deaths classified as "honor killings" are just one type of domestic violence. Others argue that there is a link between Islam and honor killings.[6] To shed light on this issue, it is important to examine the opinions of the general Muslim populace. Pew's global survey of Muslims asked respondents to what extent it is justified for family members to kill a woman, in order to protect the family's honor, who engages in premarital sex or adultery.[7]

Table 5.4 shows the percentage of Muslims in each country who responded that such killings were sometimes justified or often justified. Only in Afghanistan (60 percent) and Iraq (60 percent) do the majority endorse honor killings. However,

Table 5.4. Is it justified for family members to end a woman's life who engages in premarital sex or adultery in order to protect the family's honor?

Percent of Muslims who Responded Sometimes/Often Justified	
Afghanistan*	60%
Iraq*	60%
Jordan	41%
Lebanon	41%
Pakistan	41%
Egypt	38%
Palestinian Territories	37%
Bangladesh	36%
Tunisia	28%
Turkey	18%
Morocco	11%

*In these countries, the question was modified to: "Some people think that if a woman brings dishonor to her family it is justified for family members to end her life in order to protect the family's honor…"

in most nations a substantial minority of Muslims support honor killings, and this sheds light on the unwillingness of authorities in most of these nations to prosecute those who commit these murders. Indeed, while only 41 percent of Muslims in Pakistan approve of honor killings, they occur frequently in that nation. According to a report by the Human Rights Commission of Pakistan, 913 girls and women were known to have been honor-killed in Pakistan during 2012.[8] The report said that 604 were killed after being accused of having illicit relations with men. Another 191 were killed for marrying without the approval of their family. Interestingly enough, the Pakistan Human Rights Commission noted that seven Hindu and six Christian women also had been honor killed in that nation during 2012. Often the killings were approved by local tribal courts.

The Gallup World Poll also asked Muslim respondents in Germany, France, India, and Great Britain whether they personally believe that honor killings are morally acceptable or morally wrong. In Germany and the United Kingdom, none of the Muslims surveyed said honor killings were morally acceptable, and in France only five percent of Muslims gave that response. In India, three percent of Muslims, four percent of Hindus, and 28 percent of Sikhs believe that honor killings are morally acceptable.

Favoring Fundamentalists

Discussions of the future of the Middle East typically emphasize the conflict between the forces of modernization and those of Islamic fundamentalism. That the two are in conflict is well-known. Consider that the Qur'an strictly prohibits interest on loans (a similar Christian prohibition was reversed in the twelfth century). And for centuries the Ottoman Empire prohibited both the mechanical clock and the printing press. Perhaps of even greater significance is that Islam does not embrace the *idea of progress*. To the contrary, Islam is committed to the *idea of decline*. In addition to the Qur'an, Muslims recognize the authority of a collection of writings known as Hadith. These consist of sayings attributed to Muhammad and accounts of his actions. In the first Hadith, Muhammad is quoted: "Time has come full circle back to where it was on the day when first the heavens and earth were created." The second Hadith quotes the prophet thus: "The best generation is my generation, then the ones who follow and then those who follow them." As the Palestinian historian Tarif Khalidi interpreted, "These were both frequently cited and commented upon [by Muslim scholars]. They suggest a universe running down, an imminent end to man and all his works."[9] They also imply the superior virtue of the past. In this context, prohibiting the printing press on grounds that it is better that books be written by hand was not surprising. And of course, this contributes to the current modernist/fundamentalist conflict over the future.

The 2008 Pew Global Attitudes Survey asked respondents in five Muslim nations whether they would "be more sympathetic to the groups who want to modernize the country or Islamic fundamentalists?"[10] Table 5-5 shows how people responded.

Turkey and Lebanon are regarded as the most "secularized" Muslim states in the Middle East, and that is supported by these results—Turks and Lebanese overwhelmingly say they are more sympathetic to groups that want to modernize the country. Not so in Jordan, Egypt, and Pakistan. In all three of these nations the majority of citizens favor the fundamentalists.

Table 5-5: Sympathy for Fundamentalist or Modernist Groups.

% Muslims who favor Fundamentalists	
Jordan	59%
Egypt	55%
Pakistan	52%
Turkey	25%
Lebanon	18%

Should Shari'a Govern?

Shari'a is the moral code and religious law of Islam. Strictly speaking, it is divine law and derives from the Qur'an and by the examples set by Muhammad. Shari'a is extremely comprehensive, extending to politics and economics as well as crime, and to personal matters such as sex, hygiene, diet, prayer, and fasting. Moreover, it is considered to be infallible, to be laws directly given by Allah. It is the enforcement of Shari'a in circumstances where it is not sustained by the government that is the primary motive of Muslim terrorists. To produce, serve, or consume alcohol is a sin, hence the bombing of bars. Sex, except within marriage, is a sin, hence "honor" killings. To abandon the True Faith is an abomination. Hence, beheading neighbors suspected of reading the Bible. All other religions are false, hence attempts to blow up huge statues of Buddha and the burning of churches. Of course, as with all law, Shari'a must be interpreted and applied to particular cases, and that places immense authority in the hands of *imams* and *ulama*.

[handwritten margin note: only for women apparently]

[handwritten margin note: power]

It is the primary goal of all militant Muslim groups to establish Shari'a everywhere. What do most Muslims think about that? Table 5-6 on the following page is based on the Gallup World Polls, 2007 and 2008.

Virtually all Muslims in these Muslim nations want Shari'a to play a role in their governance, but there are marked national differences in the degree to which they want to be governed by Shari'a. Thus, while 72 percent of the Saudis want to be governed *only* by Shari'a, a mere 14 percent of Iranians agree with them—evidence that the mullahs in Iran rule a more "secular" public than is allowed to express itself in public. Many would be surprised where Egypt stands on this issue, being far more similar to Saudi Arabia, Yemen, and Afghanistan than its neighbors Libya, Algeria, and Morocco. But this is consistent with how high Egypt stands on other extremist issues already examined.

The Gallup Poll also asked this interesting question: "In principle, do you think Shari'a-based legislation should apply to both Muslims and non-Muslims or just to Muslims?" Unfortunately, the question was only asked in a somewhat odd and small selection of nations. Nevertheless, the results are shown in Table 5-7.

Table 5-6: Percent of Muslims who Think . . .

	Shari'a must be the ONLY source of legislation	Shari'a must be a source of legislation	Total
Saudi Arabia	72%	27%	99%
Qatar	70%	29%	99%
Yemen	67%	31%	98%
Egypt	67%	31%	98%
Afghanistan	67%	28%	95%
Pakistan	65%	28%	93%
Jordan	64%	35%	99%
Bangladesh	61%	33%	94%
United Arab Emirates.	57%	40%	97%
Palestinian Territories	52%	44%	96%
Iraq	49%	45%	94%
Libya	49%	44%	93%
Kuwait	46%	52%	98%
Morocco	41%	55%	96%
Algeria	37%	52%	89%
Syria	29%	57%	86%
Tunisia	24%	67%	91%
Iran	14%	70%	84%

Table 5-7: To whom should Shari'a-based legislation apply?

% Apply to both Muslims and Non-Muslims	
Bangladesh	65%
Malaysia	55%
Indonesia	51%
Pakistan	47%
Djibouti	47%
Tanzania	45%
Turkey	41%
Sierra Leone	35%
Chad	30%
Mauritania	27%
Mali	27%
Nigeria	24%
Niger	23%
Burkina Faso	21%
Senegal	9%

Here, in many Asian and African nations, Muslims are somewhat inclined not to require non-Muslims to abide by legislation based on Shari'a—although the majority do so in Bangladesh, Malaysia, and Indonesia, and near-majorities do so in Pakistan, Djibouti, Tanzania, and Turkey. No doubt support would be rather higher in the Middle East.

The "Arab" Street?

Western discussions of future relations with the Muslim world, especially concerning the prospects for "Arab Springs," often turn to the antidemocratic outbursts and mass demonstrations of what often is called the "Arab Street." The widespread assumption is that religious fanaticism is rooted primarily in the uneducated masses of Muslims and that it is they who thwart the democratic dreams of educated Muslims. This view is especially appealing to the chattering classes— especially those who do their chattering in front of college classrooms. But is it true?

Our initial doubts stemmed from knowing that many terrorists are well-educated.[11] Of course, the basis of support for extremism may, in fact, be the lower classes. Fortunately, Gallup World Poll data make it possible to discover the truth of the matter, as can be seen in Table 5-8. (Unfortunately, we could not analyze the Pew items). The results are based on all Muslims in all nations in which each question was asked.

Table 5-8: Education and Support for Extremism

	% 9/11 Justified	% Shari'a Apply to Non-Muslims	% Can't avoid conflict	% Favor Fundamentalists
No High School	22%	38%	39%	49%
High School	22%	42%	41%	40%
College	22%	42%	42%	41%

Reading down each column, we see that there are no significant educational differences in responses to these four questions. Precisely 22 percent of each educational group thinks 9/11 was justified. While 38 percent of those with less than high school educations think Shari'a ought to apply to non-Muslims as well as Muslims, so do 42 percent of those who attended high school and college. While 39 percent of those without high school educations think Muslim and Western societies cannot live together without conflict, so do 41 percent of the high school educated and 42 percent of those who went to college. Finally, Muslims without high school are slightly more likely to favor fundamentalist groups (49 percent) than are those who went to high school (40 percent) and to college (41 percent), but these differences are politically trivial. Clearly, then, it is wrong to blame Middle Eastern extremism on the Arab Street. The uneducated may be prone to demonstrate, but support for religious extremism exists at all social levels in the Muslim world.

To sum up: it is incorrect to claim that the support of religious terrorism in the Islamic world is only among small, unrepresentative cells of extremists. Granted, most citizens of

Islamic nations do not commit such acts, not even in the Middle East. But the activists do enjoy more widespread public sup- ✳ port than many have believed.

Chapter Six:
Religious Repression

In some parts of the world, religious minorities not only must fear their neighbors but also their governments. Official religious bias and repression are widespread, and many of these same governments not only fail to protect religious minorities from their neighbors, but often tacitly, and sometimes even openly, approve of mob violence and persecution. For all the horrors included in the compendium of religious atrocities, we turn now to even more unsettling matters: to religious police, to official torturers and executioners, and to rampant mobs—and sometimes armies—burning and shelling whole communities. Along the way, we also will assess milder forms of official religious bias.

Official Repression

Religious freedom exists in Saudi Arabia only to the extent that Sunni Muslims, who carefully observe every detail of Shari'a as interpreted by the eighteenth-century scholar Muhammad ibn Abd Al-Wahhab (hence "Wahhabism"), have nothing to fear from the large force of religious police. Everyone else lives in some degree of peril, as the mandate of the religious police is exceedingly broad. The 1980 law that defined their mission describes it as "guiding and advising people to observe religious duties prescribed by Islamic Shari'a and to prevent committing [acts] proscribed and prohibited [by Shari'a], or adopting bad habits and traditions or taboo heresies."[1] Thus, in addition to detecting heresy, the religious police are charged with preventing "public gender mixing and illegal private contact between men and women; practicing or displaying emblems of non-Muslim faiths or disrespecting Islam; displaying or selling media contrary to Islam, including pornography; producing, distributing, or consuming alcohol; venerating places or celebrating events inconsistent with approved Islamic practices; practicing sorcery or magic for profit;

and committing or facilitating lewdness, including adultery, homosexuality, and gambling."[2]

On June 19, 2012, a man was beheaded for "witchcraft and sorcery"—the first "fruit" of a vigorous new campaign the religious police have launched against "sorcerers." Indeed, all public school students receive mandatory instruction that includes directives "to kill sorcerers." Saudi Arabian students also are taught that the killing of Islamic minorities and "apostates" is justified—an official eighth-grade textbook states, "The Apes are the people of the Sabbath, the Jews; the Swine are the infidels of the communion of Jesus, the Christians."[3]

Private schools that depart from these official interpretations of Islam are not permitted. The Shi'ah Muslim minority is permitted to have mosques, but they often have great difficulty in gaining building permits, and they must play the Sunni call to prayer over their public address systems, which is somewhat different from the Shi'ah call. Public worship by anyone other than Sunni or Shi'ah Muslims is strictly forbidden. Nor is it even safe to hold worship services in private—although it is officially permitted. On August 1, 2012, thirty-five Ethiopian Christians were deported for worshipping as a group in private.[4] Other groups detected holding private services have been "flogged, beaten, jailed ... or even killed."[5] And leading imams continue to pray during services, even in the most celebrated mosques, for the deaths of Christians and Jews.

It would be extremely difficult to sustain a state more repressive of religious freedom than Saudi Arabia, but the rulers of Myanmar, also known as Burma, may have succeeded. In part this is because, aside from the Shi'ah, there are hardly any religious nonconformists in Saudi Arabia available for attacks. But in Myanmar, the repressive regime which holds that the nation is a Buddhist state, has millions of Christians and Muslims to victimize. Worse yet, both the Christians and the Muslims also constitute minority ethnic groups and are hated by the majority on those grounds, as well. Hence, the official policy is "One Race, One Language, One Religion." In this spirit, the army has burned whole areas and driven out huge numbers of Christians and Muslims. Of course, it is illegal to import Bibles or Qur'ans or to build or rebuild churches or mosques.

The governments of Saudi Arabia and Myanmar are repressive defenders of their one true faith, but the government of North Korea is a repressive offender of every faith—it "is the most militantly atheistic country in the world."[6] All religious activity is forbidden, and anyone suspected of being a believer in any religion is very likely to be sent to a labor camp, if not murdered—as was a middle-aged Chinese woman, recently discovered to have a Bible in her home, who was seized by government agents, tied to a stake, and shot.[7]

Much of the above information about religious repression comes from the 2013 *U.S. State Department Report on International Religious Freedom*, issued annually on the basis of careful reports filed by each American embassy around the world and augmented by official sources for nations with whom the U.S. does not have diplomatic relations. Several years ago, Brian J. Grim and Roger Finke coded the report for 2003 to create three very useful indices.[8] The first index measures government repression of religion.[9] It is based on these six factors:

1. Are foreign missionaries permitted to operate?

2. Is religious proselytizing, public preaching, or conversion limited or restricted?

3. Does the government interfere with an individual's right to worship?

4.   Are there legal or practical protections for freedom of religion?

5. Does the government generally respect freedom of religion?

6. Does government policy contribute to freedom of religion?

Each of these factors was assigned one point and the result multiplied to produce a scale from zero through ten—the higher the score, the higher the level of government repression of religion. Grim and Finke subsequently updated this index based on the 2008 report. Starting with Grim and Finke's 2008 coding, we revised their scores on the basis of the 2013 report, which assessed conditions in 2012. Table 6-1 shows the twenty-five nations with the highest scores on government repression of religion.

Table 6-1: Top 25 Nations on Religious Repression Index and Percent Muslim

Nation Repression	Score	Percent Muslim
Saudi Arabia	10	99%
Iran	10	99%
Myanmar (Burma)	10	4%
North Korea	10	0%
Afghanistan	10	99%
China	9.8	1%
Maldives	9.6	99%
Pakistan	9.5	95%
Brunei	9.4	67%
Jordan	9.4	92%
Comoros	9.4	98%
Egypt	9.2	90%
Eritrea	9.1	51%
Uzbekistan	9.0	88%
Libya	8.6	97%
Somalia	8.6	99%
Malaysia	8.6	60%
Vietnam	8.6	0.1%
Turkmenistan	8.6	89%
Azerbaijan	8.6	93%
Tunisia	8.6	98%
Algeria	8.6	99%
Syria	8.4	80%
Kuwait	7.8	85%
Tajikistan	7.8	90%

Except for Myanmar, North Korea, China, and Vietnam, the other twenty-one nations in the top twenty-five states most repressive of religion are overwhelmingly Muslim. Some might argue that Muslim nations score high, not because of their religious outlook, but merely because they aren't democracies. However, that assumes that their being Muslim plays no role in their lack of democracy—a very dubious assumption, given the extensive emphasis by leading imams that democracy is another form of Western decadence and is incompatible with Islam.

Nor does democracy always sustain toleration. Consider these findings. Recently the Gallup World Poll asked people in forty-six nations whether or not they would agree or disagree with a constitutional provision that gave "Freedom of religion—allowing all citizens to observe any religion of their choice and to practice its teachings and beliefs." Table 6-2 reports the Gallup findings.

Table 6-2: Opposition to Religious Freedom

Nation	% Opposed
Libya	72%
Saudi Arabia	65%
Yemen	63%
Comoros	57%
Afghanistan	55%
Somalia	49%
Jordan	46%
Algeria	44%
West Bank	42%
United Arab Emirates	40%
Morocco	35%
Oman	34%
Egypt	33%
Kuwait	25%
Mauritania	24%
Iraq	24%

Table 6-2: Opposition to Religious Freedom (cont.)

Nation	% Opposed
Iran	23%
Qatar	23%
Djibouti	22%
Syria	21%
Tajikistan	15%
Pakistan	14%
Kyrgyzstan	14%
Malaysia	14%
Tunisia	13%
Albania	13%
Sudan	13%
Uzbekistan	13%
India	13%
Kazakhstan	11%
Niger	11%
Tanzania	10%
Azerbaijan	10%
Sierra Leone	9%
Indonesia	8%
Senegal	8%
Guinea	8%
Chad	8%
Ethiopia	7%
Turkey	7%
Burkina Faso	7%
Bosnia	7%
Mali	6%
Lebanon	6%
Bangladesh	5%
Nigeria	3%

There is far less opposition to religious freedom in many Muslim nations than might have been supposed. Of course, it is one thing to agree with religious freedom in principle, but another to support it in practice—it would have been nice to have data on willingness to permit the public sale of Bibles or the visible display of statues of Buddha. In fact, many Muslim leaders claim that non-Muslims are entirely free to practice their religion—if they do so in private.

Official Bias

Obviously there is no separation of church and state when governments suppress religious liberty. And while North Korea, and to a lesser extent China, seek to suppress all faiths, most of the other very repressive states act for the benefit of what they regard as the one true faith. However, governments can be considerably biased in favor of a particular faith without resorting to religious police or other extreme measures—practicing instead a genteel sort of discrimination, but effective nonetheless.

In most European nations, there is nothing resembling a separation of church and state. True, European governments are not vigorously repressive. But in many of them, there are established state churches supported by taxes. In most of the rest, a particular religion is the object of considerable government "favoritism." And in nearly all European nations, the government bureaucracy engages in overt and covert interference with all religious "outsiders" and "newcomers" that challenge the established religious order.

There are Lutheran state churches in Denmark, Finland, Iceland, and Norway, while in Sweden, the established position of the Church of Sweden (Lutheran) was ended in 2006, although the government continues to collect a religious tax on its behalf. There are two state churches in Germany, the Evangelical Church (Protestant) and the Roman Catholic Church, both supported by taxes and their clergy classified as civil servants. Some cantons in Switzerland recognize Roman Catholicism as the state church; other cantons support an Evangelical Reformed state church. The Roman Catholic Church receives tax support in Austria and payments of more than six billion Euros a year in Spain. In Italy, people choose the group to receive their church tax from a short list of Christian denominations, and in Belgium there is no church tax, but the government provides very substantial support to Catholicism, Protestantism, Anglicanism, Judaism, Islam, and a category called "nondenominational." There is no church tax in the Netherlands, but the two primary Protestant churches and the Roman Catholics receive many large subsidies. No religious group receives direct government support in France, but the Catholic schools receive huge subsidies, and immense favoritism is shown to the Roman Catholic Church by the bureaucracy. Finally, the Church of England remains the established faith but is not supported by taxes or government funds, being able to sustain itself from huge endowments built up during prior centuries of mandatory tithing.

These close links between church and state have many consequences. First of all, they create lazy churches. The money continues to come whether or not people attend, so there is no need for clergy to exert themselves. Second, these links encourage people to view religion "as a type of public utility."[10] Individuals need do nothing to preserve the church; the government will see to it. This attitude makes it difficult for nonsubsidized faiths to compete—people will be reluctant to contribute to a church. Thus, when some German evangelists attempted television ministries, they drew viewers but not contributions,[11] since religion is supposed to come free.

The existence of favored churches also encourages government hindrance and harassment of other churches. The French government has officially designated 173 religious groups (most of them evangelical Protestants, including Baptists) as dangerous cults, imposing heavy tax burdens upon them and subjecting their members to official discrimination in such things as employment. Subsequently, Belgium has outdone the French, identifying 189 dangerous cults, including the Quakers, the YWCA (but not the YMCA), Hasidic Jews, Assemblies of God, the Amish, Buddhists, and Seventh-Day Adventists.

But even groups not condemned by parliamentary action are targets of government interference. As the distinguished British sociologist James Beckford noted, all across Europe government bureaucrats impose "administrative sanctions . . . behind a curtain of official detachment."[12] Many Protestant groups report waiting for years to obtain a building permit for a church, or even for a permit to allow an existing building to

as in Calgary, Canada

be used as a church. This is especially common in Scandina-
vian nations, where it is often ruled that there is "no need" for
an additional church in some area, hence no permit is granted.[13]
In Germany, many Pentecostal groups have been denied tax-
free status unless they register with the government as secular
groups such as sports clubs rather than as churches. Subsequently, the government sometimes revokes their tax exempt
status and imposes unpayable fines and back tax demands on
congregations.[14]

Nevertheless, many European scholars are adamant that
their nations enjoy full religious liberty. To challenge that claim,
it no longer is necessary to recite examples of state intrusions,
because Brian Grim and Roger Finke[15] have created a quanti-
tative index of government favoritism in religious life. This index was created from the U.S. State Department's *International
Religious Freedom Report* as was the Religious Repression Index examined above. On the latter, most European nations
appear to offer a fair amount of religious freedom, most of
them scoring zero on the repression index. But Grim and
Finke's *Government Favoritism Index* tells a very different story.

The favoritism index is based on "subsidies, privileges, support, or favorable sanctions provided by the state to a select
religion or a small group of religions."[16] This index also varies
from 0.0 (no favoritism) to 10.0 (extreme favoritism). The
United States and Taiwan score 0.0, while Saudi Arabia and
Iran each score 9.3. And although Afghanistan and the United
Arab Emirates score 7.8, so do Iceland, Spain, and Greece,
while Belgium scores 7.5, slightly higher than Bangladesh's
7.3 and India's 7.0. Morocco scores 6.3, while Denmark scores
6.7, Finland, 6.5, Austria 6.2, Switzerland 5.8, France 5.5, Italy,
5.3, and Norway 5.2.

Clearly, Europe is quite lacking in the separation of church
and state, and in ways that are considerably biased against
most faiths. In fact, European public opinion is rather supportive of restrictions on religious expression. The Gallup World
Poll asked, "Different people have different opinions about
displaying religious symbols in public spaces such as schools
in this country. I will read you a list of religious symbols, and
you tell me if you think it is a good idea or a bad idea to ban
these in public spaces." The question was only asked in three
nations, but the results are revealing nonetheless.

Table 6-3: Should these religious symbols be banned in public spaces?

	Percent should be Banned
Face Veils	
France	76%
Germany	59%
Great Britain	51%
Muslim Headscarves	
France	76%
Germany	48%
Great Britain	29%
Jewish Yarmulkes	
France	74%
Germany	34%
Great Britain	19%
Sikh Turbans	
France	72%
Germany	37%
Great Britain	15%
Christian Crosses	
France	61%
Germany	26%
Great Britain	11%

The French are overwhelmingly opposed to the public wearing of religious symbols, whether face veils or Christian crosses. And, of course, the French parliament did outlaw the covering of the face in any public space, leading to riots in 2013—but the French did not relax the law. A majority of Germans would ban the veil, a near majority would ban the Muslim headscarf, a third would prohibit yarmulkes and turbans, and one of four Germans would also outlaw the wearing of crosses. The British are more liberal on these matters, although half would ban the veil.

Social Pressure

Even in societies where the government scrupulously sustains religious freedom, there may be considerable pressure toward religious conformity exerted by the public. As noted in Chapter 4, even in the United States atheists feel themselves somewhat stigmatized, as do Evangelical Christians, and not so very long ago there was significant discrimination against Catholics and Jews. Of course, in societies where the government represses minority religions, the public is likely to do so, as well. Grim and Finke attempted to codify this aspect of societies, applying these standards:

1. Prevalence of negative attitudes toward other or nontraditional religions.

2. Negative attitudes toward conversion to other religions.

3. Negative attitudes toward proselytizing.

4. Prevalence of social movements against nonconforming religions.

Grim and Finke's Index of Social Regulation of Religion also ranges from zero to ten: the higher the score, the greater the social pressure for religious conformity that exists in a nation. We have modified and updated their coding to create an *Index of Religious Social Pressure*. Thus, for example, while the United States is properly scored 0.0 on state repression, we scored it as 2.0 on social pressure, although Grim and Finke had scored it 0.0 on their measure. We based our decision on the assumption that religious social pressure is a matter of degree, not the total absence of any social pressure for religious conformity in any nation. For example, there are a substantial number of Americans who have religious objections to the lyrics of some contemporary music, and who have sometimes tried to prevent such material from being played on the radio. That constitutes religious social pressure, albeit these Americans are not inclined to behead any pop performers, let alone those who listen to pop music. But there were several such incidents included in the Index of Atrocities in which Muslims beheaded or otherwise murdered fellow Muslims for listening to or dancing to Western pop music. In any event, although Grim and Finke coded a number of other nations as 0.0 on their measure of social regulation, we thought it more realistic to code these nations as 1.0, not that it makes any statistical difference.

Table 6-4 shows the twenty-five nations scored highest on social pressure as well as the percent Muslim.

Twenty-three of the top twenty-five are overwhelmingly Muslim nations. As for the two exceptions, Indian Hindus and Ethiopian Christians have experienced centuries of conflict with local Muslims.

For further insight into the social climate surrounding religious minorities, the Gallup World Poll asked, "Is the city or area where you live a good place or not a good place to live for religious minorities?" Table 6-5 reveals the thirty nations scoring highest as *not* a good place to live for religious minorities, and also the ten nations scoring lowest.

We have no idea why Cambodians are so inclined to believe that where they live would not be a good place for religious minorities—not a single one of the 810 incidents included in our Atrocities Index occurred in Cambodia, and the State Department noted that there "were no reports of societal abuses or discrimination based on religious affiliation, belief, or practice"[17] in Cambodia. Laos is less of a mystery—the Laotian government has been harassing Christians recently. Even so, on objective grounds Laos would be a far better place for religious minorities to live than, say, Saudi Arabia, but the overwhelming majority of Saudi Arabians think theirs is a good place for religious minorities to live. Perhaps Saudis are influenced by the fact that Christians living in the enclosed communities for Western petroleum technologists are entirely safe. And perhaps they were merely being patriotic as, no doubt,

Table 6-4: Top 25 Nations on Religious Social Pressure Index and Percent Muslim

Nation	Social Pressure Score	Percent Muslim
Afghanistan	10	99%
Egypt	10	90%
Gaza Strip	10	99%
India	10	13%
Iran	10	99%
Pakistan	10	95%
Saudi Arabia	10	99%
West Bank	10	75%
Syria	9.6	80%
Maldives	9.5	99%
Indonesia	9.3	86%
Azerbaijan	9.3	93%
Iraq	9.3	97%
Libya	9.2	97%
Chad	8.8	53%
Somalia	8.8	99%
Tunisia	8.8	98%
Ethiopia	8.7	34%
Uzbekistan	8.7	88%
Bangladesh	8.5	90%
Comoros	8.5	98%
Morocco	8.3	99%
Kuwait	8.3	85%
Algeria	8.3	99%
Turkey	8.3	99%

Table 6-5: Thirty highest and 10 lowest in percent responding "not a good place [for religious minorities] to live."

Cambodia	72%	Sierra Leone	38%
Laos	65%	Morocco	38%
Jordan	59%	Indonesia	37%
Thailand	56%	Moldova	36%
West Bank	54%	Ethiopia	36%
Japan	50%	Austria	36%
Armenia	49%	South Korea	35%
Pakistan	48%	Czech Republic	35%
Israel	44%	Poland	34%
Rwanda	44%	Saudi Arabia	34%
Iran	43%	Slovenia	34%
Kyrgyzstan	41%	Chad	33%
Georgia	39%	Sudan	33%
Tanzania	39%	Turkey	33%
Greece	38%	Russia	33%
Lowest			
United States	10%	Namibia	9%
Nepal	10%	Australia	9%
Guyana	10%	Burkina Faso	9%
Canada	9%	Brazil	9%
Senegal	9%	New Zealand	8%

were many others who thought that theirs was a good place for religious minorities to live.

To bring everything together, Table 6-5 shows the correlations among these four measures and the percent Christian and Muslim.

As indicated in the tables, religious repression is highly positively correlated with the percent Muslim in a nation's population, and negatively with the percent Christian. Official and social repression are very highly correlated (.74), and both are correlated with being opposed to religious freedom.

To sum up, real religious freedom is lacking in most of the world.

Table 6-5: Correlations Among the Measures of Religious Repression.

	Official Rep.	Gov't Fav.	Social Rep.	Anti-Rel. Freedom.
% Christian	-.59**	-.15*	-51**	-.45**
% Muslim	.65**	.31**	.61**	.50**
Official Repression		.36**	.74**	.56**
Government Favoritism			.49**	.25*
Social Repression				.42**

** < .01   * < .05

Chapter Seven: Religious Refugees

Once again an Exodus or two, or three, or many more. This time it isn't only Jews, but also Christians who are fleeing. Christians are leaving North Africa and the Middle East to escape vindictive <u>Muslim</u> majorities. Jews are leaving Europe to escape vindictive <u>Muslim</u> minorities. And even where governments are not part of the problem, they are contributing little or nothing to any solution. It is a depressing sight.

Christian Exodus from Islam

Although Christianity is the largest, most rapidly growing faith in the world, it is in the process of disappearing from some nations—not because Christians are converting to other religions, but because they are being driven out. Much has been written about this recently, some stories based on sensational but inaccurate statistics, and others, while offering highly reliable and readable anecdotes, lack in statistics.[1] We shall try to correct these deficiencies, but readers should be warned that rates of Christian flight from any particular nation can change dramatically within a few months.

Estimating Christian Fatalities

Several weeks before we planned to begin this chapter, headlines across the world reported that "one hundred thousand Christians are killed every year for their faith." The source was the Vatican, where Archbishop Silvano Maria Tomasi, who released the figures, called them "shocking" and "incredible."

We, too, were shocked, and we also found the number incredible, but for rather different reasons. How could such a figure be possible? The incidents coded in our Atrocity Index involved only 1,045 Christian deaths in 2012. Of course, that number was extremely conservative given our rules for including an incident as religiously motivated. But even if all the

[handwritten marginal note: are we blamed the crusaders?]

Christian deaths in all terrorist incidents we examined were included, the total number would not exceed four thousand. If we added, as a very generous estimate, another two thousand for deaths from government attacks, as in Myanmar, the total still would not exceed six thousand. Where are the other ninety-four thousand? More specifically, where are the incidents adding up to this huge total? It seems implausible that the world press could have missed a whole series of very major massacres. Yet, to reach such a huge total, many such events would be required.

As we pursued the matter,[2] we discovered that the Vatican was not the source of the claim. Archbishop Tomasi was quoting an estimate published by the Center for the Study of Global Christianity at the Gordon-Conwell Theological Seminary in South Hamilton, MA. Indeed, this was not the first time the researchers at Gordon-Conwell had claimed a huge Christian martyrdom rate—they had proposed 176,000 deaths per year in 2009, 178,000 in 2010, and 100,000 in 2011.

When we inquired as to the basis for these estimates of Christian fatalities, we were told that they were not specific to any given year, but that each was an average based on the total number of deaths during the previous ten years. The criterion for counting a death was that "believers in Christ . . . lost their lives, prematurely, in situations of witness, as a result of human hostility." Some of these deaths, then, would have been due to illness and starvation that might have been prevented. Moreover, although use of a ten-year average was intended to iron out random statistical variations from year-to-year, such an average can be exceedingly misleading. For example, if applied to deaths in the United States due to terrorist attacks, then for the decade 2001-2011, an average of three hundred Americans were killed annually. But, in many of those years, no one in the United States was killed by terrorists; the average was based entirely on those who died in the single 9/11 incident. To thus claim an average of three hundred deaths per year borders on committing a hoax.

However, the worst fallacy involved in the claim of one hundred thousand or more Christian deaths per year was to include in the total to be averaged the eight hundred thousand or so deaths that occurred in the Rwandan genocide, as well as the millions killed in the civil war that raged in the

Congo. Granted that most who died in these great tragedies were Christians, there is no evidence that a significant number of these people died *because* they were Christians. If these people count as martyrs, then so do all Christians everywhere in the world who died untimely deaths for whatever reason— more than twenty thousand American Christians became martyrs every year in auto accidents! To put things bluntly, the claim of one hundred thousand Christian martyrs a year is not only absurd; it threatens to discredit claims about a truly serious matter—that, in fact, Christians are being brutalized and threatened in many nations.

Thomas Schirrmacher, a German sociologist and theologian, proposes that about seven thousand Christians are being martyred annually,[3] which strikes us as plausible, if perhaps a bit high. In any event, what is clear is that it doesn't take a huge number of deaths, when combined with beatings, rapes, arson, and public threats, to cause people to flee. And of that there can be no doubt: a new exodus of Christians is underway, especially from North Africa and the Middle East.

Christian Refugees

There are widespread reports of Christians fleeing and being driven out of Islamic nations. The U.S. Commission on International Religious Freedom reported, "The flight of Christians out of the region is unprecedented, and it's increasing year by year. ... [soon] Christians might disappear altogether from Iraq, Afghanistan, and Egypt."[4] As for Syria, according to the *New York Times*, of the eighty thousand Christians who lived in the city of Homs two years ago, "approximately four hundred remain today."[5] And then there is Egypt, where no recent government seems inclined to protect the more than ten million Christian Copts—a community dating back to the days of the Roman Empire. Long before muslims lived there

We have no doubt that a massive exodus of Christians is taking place, but it has been extremely difficult to find any trustworthy statistics. We suspect that the claims reported above are far more trustworthy than the claim that one hundred thousand or more Christians are martyred every year, but we wanted to base our analysis on more solid statistics. Fortunately, we found some quite reliable statistics—their only shortcoming having to do with their being several years old.

Thus, although these statistics cannot reflect the massive new exodus from Syria or a departure of Copts, they are highly revealing nonetheless.

The data were collected by the Pew Research Center and published in 2012.[6] The Pew report gives an estimate of the total number of emigrants and their religious makeup from each nation as of 2010. That makes it possible not only to know the number of Christians leaving each nation, but by comparing the percentage of Christians among the emigrants with the percentage of Christians in each nation's population, to calculate whether or not Christians are departing in disproportionate numbers. For example, assume that Christians made up 10 percent of a particular nation's emigrants as of 2010. Then, if Christians also constituted 10 percent of the population, the Christian emigration rate was at precisely their expected share. But, if Christians made up only 2 percent of that nation's population, then its Christian emigration rate was five times higher than their expected share.

For each nation discussed below, we shall start with such a calculation of Christian emigration. In some cases we will add more recent reports suggesting a massive increase in Christian flight since the statistics on emigration became available. Some nations that are notorious for repressing religious minorities do not appear below because their Christian populations already are so tiny that they do not generate statistics. Among these are Afghanistan, Algeria, Bangladesh, Morocco, Niger, Somalia, Tunisia, and Yemen.

Nations discussed below are ordered according to their estimated level of Christian flight. Only nations with Christian emigration rates at least 2.0 times their expected share are included (except for Egypt, as is explained).

Iran—Christian emigration: *21.6 times* expected share.

There are fewer than three hundred thousand Christians remaining in this nation of 78 million. Nearly all of these are ethnic Armenians, belonging to the Armenian Apostolic Church. By law, all Christian worship must be in the Assyrian or Armenian languages, a rule that is meant to prevent any efforts to convert Iran's Farsi-speaking Muslims. The secret police are vigorous in seeking out violators, and those whom they discover are severely punished. In addition to raiding churches and charging Christians with all manner of misdeeds, in 2011 the government prohibited the celebration of Christmas and ordered the churches to instead support a Shi'ah Muslim period of mourning. The basic government view of Christians was expressed by Ayatollah Ahmed Jannati, who denounced them as "animals who roam the Earth and engage in corruption."[7] Little wonder that Christians with anywhere to go, do.

Turkey—Christian emigration: *11.1 times* **expected share.**

Turkish law restricts all religious services to a legal house of worship. "Authorities have approved only one new Christian church as a place of worship since the founding of the republic in 1923."[8] The Syrian Orthodox community in Istanbul, with an estimated membership of 20,000, has only one church despite having sought for decades to obtain a permit to build a second. As for Protestants, they have only fifteen churches throughout the country, most of them being small chapels serving foreign diplomats. Consequently, Protestants are forced to worship in private homes, for which they sometimes are arrested. And that is precisely why Christians leave Turkey, despite constitutional protections for religious liberty. Although the Turks do interfere with Muslim freedoms, too, Turkey is a Muslim nation, and the religious climate has been increasingly influenced by the rise of Islamic militancy in the region. Granted that there have been no anti-Christian riots and terrorist attacks are rare—we discovered only one in 2012 for inclusion in the Atrocities Index. But there has been an occasional murder of a Christian leader, for which the prosecutors and courts have been very lenient on the perpetrators.[9]

Iraq—Christian emigration: *7.8 times* **expected share.**

Iraq is second only to Pakistan on our Atrocities Index, and many of these attacks were directed against Christians. Nor were these mostly incidents involving a death or two; Iraq's terrorists specialize in massacres.

- *October 31, 2010*: During Sunday Mass at Our Sister of Perpetual Help, a Catholic Church in Baghdad, terrorists burst in and shot down fifty-six worshippers and two priests, leaving another priest and more than sixty worshippers wounded. More often, however, massive casualties have been inflicted by car bombs in Christian neighborhoods or outside Christian businesses.

Despite the powerful American military and diplomatic presence, the government has not been very committed to religious freedom. Islam is the official religion, and the constitution states that no legislation may be passed that contradicts any provisions of Islamic law. By far the majority of attacks involve Muslims against Muslims, and most of the casualties are Muslims, too. Consequently, the great majority of the more than a million Iraqi refugees are Muslims, as well.[10] But proportionately, Christians have borne the greater brunt of terrorism, and their flight continues. In 2009 and again in 2010, the Gallup World Poll asked people in Iraq, "Within the past twelve months, have you been assaulted or mugged?" Combining the two years in order to have an adequate number of Christians, an astonishing 15 percent of Christians said yes, as did 10 percent of Muslims.

Azerbaijan—Christian emigration: *6.5 times* expected share.

Located between Russia and Iran, with a coastline along the Caspian Sea, this Muslim nation became an independent republic in 1991 upon the collapse of the Soviet Union. The small number of Christians are mostly members of the Russian Orthodox or Armenian Apostolic Churches, and they live mainly in the largest cities. All religious groups are tightly regulated—prior government approval is even required for the printing or distribution of all religious literature. Christian proselytization is strictly forbidden and has often resulted in arrest and imprisonment. Currently there is considerable emigration from this small nation of 9.4 million, with Christians making up a very disproportionate share of those leaving.

Bahrain—Christian emigration: *5.1 times* expected share.

This tiny nation on the Persian Gulf, nestled against Saudi Arabia, has been called "the most tolerant nation on the Arabian Peninsula."[11] Yet it has a Christian emigration rate of 5.1 times the expected rate. That's partly because of the intense hostility toward Christians in the immediate region, and partly because the religious climate has recently become far more uncomfortable in Bahrain. The primary focus of religious conflict is between the Sunni and the Shi'ah, with violent incidents becoming increasingly frequent. As would be expected, persecution of Christians often is a byproduct of the increased level of religious antagonism within the Muslim community.

India—Christian emigration: *4.1 times* expected share.

In November 2012, the Indian Ministry of Home Affairs reported that in the previous nine months there had been 560 cases of communal violence based on religious differences, causing eighty-nine deaths and 1,846 injuries.[12] Twenty of the fatal incidents are included in our Atrocity Index.

Although India has a long and tragic record of religious violence between Muslims and Hindus, the small Christian population has increasingly become the target of Hindu extremists, often abetted by the local police. Paul Marshall and his co-authors report twelve vicious Hindu attacks on Christians that took place during the one-month period of December 2011. Among them:

- *December 8*: Hindu extremists attack and beat three Christian families. When the Christians complain to the police, they (not their attackers) are arrested.

- *December 22*: Hindu terrorists burn down a church in order to prevent Christmas services. When students from a local college organize a Christmas program, they are arrested.

Most Indian states have laws prohibiting forced conversions, and the police and courts often impose these statutes even when all of the converts deny their conversions were forced.

- *December 18*: A mob of about two hundred Hindu extremists burst into a Baptist church during Sunday services and severely beat the two pastors, accusing them of forced conversions. The police come and arrest the pastors and then question about twnety persons who allegedly had been forced to become Christians. All of them vigorously deny that claim. So instead, the police charge the pastors with "promoting enmity between different groups on grounds of religion."[13]

In addition, some attacks on Christians in India are by Muslim terrorists.

- *October 14, 2012*: Two Christians are shot to death in their home by Muslims attempting to kidnap and convert their daughter.

- *March 30, 2012*: A sixty-five-year-old Christian widow is badly beaten in her church by Islamic extremists.

Consequently, Indian Christians are more likely than other Indians to emigrate, and those with technical educations often come to the United States—a third of the engineers in California's Silicon Valley are immigrants from India.[14]

Muslims also are victims of violence in India, usually at the hands of other Muslims.

- *August 10, 2012*: An elderly Muslim man is shot outside a mosque by gunmen belonging to the Islamic Movement of Kashmir.

- *March 19, 2013*: Militant Muslims shoot an eighteen-year-old to death in a mosque.

According to the Gallup World Poll (combined results from the 2006 through 2010 surveys), 7 percent of Christians and 6 percent of Muslims in India report that they have been assaulted or mugged in the past year.

China—Christian emigration: *3.7 times* expected share.

Everyone agrees that Christianity is growing very rapidly in China. In 1949 when the Communists came to power, there were an estimated million Chinese Christians. Then came decades of vicious repression, during which the number of Christians seems to have grown! And once the repression eased, Christian growth accelerated. The best study shows that there were about sixty-five million Christians over age sixteen in China in 2007.[15] Hence there probably are at least seventy-five million Chinese Christians today. Perhaps even more interesting is that Christianity does not appeal mainly to the poor or the peasants, but to the best-educated, upper-income Chinese—Christians abound on the elite university campuses. Even so, the government continues to impose sanctions against religion—not only Christianity, but Islam and even Buddhism—while pretending that Confucianism is not a religion, despite the crowds praying to statues of Confucius in the many temples devoted to him.[16]

All religious groups are required to register with the government, and not all are awarded permits. Large numbers of Christian groups remain unregistered—organized as "house churches." Most of the time, the government overlooks the house churches, but often enough they raid them and even send their pastors to labor camps. The U.S. State Department in its 2013 *International Freedom Report* noted that the Chinese "government harassed, detained, arrested, and sentenced to prison a number of religious adherents for activities reportedly related to their religious beliefs and practice."[17] In response to such criticism from abroad, the Chinese government explains that no one is punished for their religious faith, but only for breaking the law. Of course, as Marshall and his co-authors point out, this "fails to acknowledge that their laws criminalize peaceful religious acts protected by international human rights agreements."[18]

Little wonder that Chinese Christians are inclined to leave if they can.

Myanmar (Burma)—Christian emigration: *3.4 times* **expected share (not counting huge numbers in refugee camps).**

Since 1999, Myanmar has been designated as a "Country of Particular Concern" by the U.S. State Department under the International Religious Freedom Act. As noted in Chapter 6, the primary "terrorists" attacking religious minorities in Myanmar are regular army units, who have murdered and dispossessed huge numbers of Muslims and Christians, most of whom also are members of despised ethnic groups, such as the Karen. Vision Beyond Borders reported in 2009, "Villages are being surrounded, and rockets lobbed in. The Myanmar regime then goes in with machine guns and mows down whoever is still alive, and then the evidence is burned."[19] According to the U.S. State Department 2013 report, military violence in Rakhine State killed "an estimated 250 people and led to the displacement of more than one hundred thousand."[20] It is estimated that there are at least five hundred thousand Christian and Muslim refugees living in camps within Myanmar and several million more in camps across the borders in Thailand, China, India, and Bangladesh. All of this is done in the name of one true faith: Buddhism.

Of course, such government activity spurs on the citizenry, too:

- *May 2, 2013*: One Muslim is killed and ten are injured as a Buddhist mob attacks two mosques and burn Muslim neighborhoods.

Thailand—Christian emigration: *2.5 times* expected share.

Thailand scored very high on our Atrocities Index, with fifty-two fatal attacks known to have taken place during 2012. Religious violence in Thailand usually involves Muslims attacking Buddhists, despite the fact that the nation is 93 percent Buddhist and only 5 percent Muslim.

- *February 5, 2012*: Muslim gunmen ambush a group of Buddhist monks, killing two.

- *September 21, 2012*: Muslim terrorists kill six and injure forty by exploding a car bomb near a Buddhist-owned business that had remained open on an Islamic holy day.

In addition, there were "at least ninety-nine incidents during the month [of Ramadan in 2012], killing fifty-two and injuring ninety-eight others." [21]

However, even though the Christian population is very small, both Buddhists and Muslims find occasions to attack them. In November 2012 "a group of approximately twenty Buddhist villagers in Udon Thani province stormed a Christian church and destroyed its contents." [22] And in April 2012, Muslims bombed a Christian community center, killing two.

Jordan—Christian emigration: *2.5 times* expected share.

The small Christian minority in Jordan has not suffered from terrorist attacks, nor has it been subjected to discrimination—Christians often serve as cabinet ministers and achieve high ranks in the army. But because Shari'a law takes precedence, there is constant tension over the forbidden act of conversion. Although Jordanians do not execute Muslims who convert to Christianity (as happens in some Islamic nations), they often resort to deporting them against their will. Probably in order to detect converts or other violations of Shari'a, plainclothes security officers often observe Christian churches.[23]

Syria—Christian emigration: *2.3 times* expected share (*14 times* when adjusted for the recent huge increase, see below).

Until the civil war broke out in 2011, Christians were fairly secure in Syria. This was not because the state truly supported religious freedom—there were and are many restrictions on non-Muslims—but because the government suppressed religious conflicts. It did so because, although Sunnis make up the overwhelming majority of Syrians, the authoritarian regime is controlled by members of the Alawi Muslim sect, which broke off from the Shi'ah in the eighth century and whose members have often been persecuted in other Islamic nations. Thus, it was in the interest of President Bashar al-Assad and his inner circle to suppress all Muslim "extremists" and civil disturbances. However, once the civil war broke out, extremists came to the fore on both sides. Antigovernment forces are dominated by the Muslim Brotherhood and groups such as al-Qaeda; government forces are backed by "volunteers" from Iran and by the terrorist group Hezbollah. Consequently, both sides soon began attacking Christians as opportunities arose, purely as a matter of ideology, since neither side seems to have anything to gain from driving out the Christians.

As a result, a huge Christian exodus has begun. According to the *New York Times*, as of June 2013, Lebanon had officially received 546,000 Syrian refugees, most of them Christians, and the government estimates that another 500,000 Syrian refugees have not registered—they are scattered in fourteen hundred locations. Jordan had accepted 478,000 Syrians, 386,000 had fled to Turkey, 158,000 to Iraq, and 81,000 to Egypt.[24] Little wonder that the Christian sections of Syria's cities are ghost towns.

Libya—Christian emigration: *2.1 times* expected share.

The eruption of civil war in Libya during February 2011 was greeted joyfully in Western nations—the tyrannical rule of Muammar Gadhafi was soon to end with the triumph of an "Arab Spring." The United Nations Security Council backed the rebels as did most European nations and the United States, not merely with words, but eventually with arms. But the new government was soon revealed as another repressive Muslim state, committed to Shari'a and willing to condone persecution of religious minorities, especially Christians. Indeed, in October 2012, the Grand Mufti called upon the Ministry of Education "to remove passages relating to religious freedom from school textbooks, because it suggested to young students that they were free to choose any religion."[25]

Two months later anti-Christian terrorism began.

- *December 29, 2012*: A bomb was exploded next to a Coptic Orthodox Church during Sunday Services, killing two and injuring three.

- *March 15, 2013*: The Associated Press reported that about fifty Coptic Christians had been seized in a marketplace and taken to a detention center run by a government-sponsored militia. There they had their heads shaved and were tortured at length, at least one of them fatally.

There have now been many such events. Indeed, several days after the AP story broke, the head of the human rights committee of the Libyan parliament fled to London, where he told the press that he had observed abuses taking place that were "much worse than those that took place in the days of Gadhafi."[26]

Subsequently, in September 2012, Libyan television carried a sermon from a mosque in Benghazi that called on Allah to "destroy the rancorous Christians and the corrupt Jews."[27]

Malaysia—Christian emigration: *2.1 times* expected share.

Hostility toward Christianity has been encouraged by recent, frequent claims by government officials that there is a plot afoot to make Malaysia into a Christian nation—despite the fact that Christians make up only 9 percent of the population. To "prevent" such a thing from happening, Christians are prohibited from using the word *Allah*, and all Bibles must have "For Christians Only" stamped on their covers. The government also maintains religious rehabilitation centers to which individuals who are suspected of apostasy, or those who actually have converted from Islam, are sentenced.[28] However, religious violence is rare—there are no incidents from Malaysia in the Atrocities Index.

Egypt—Christian emigration: *1.6 times* expected share (at least *3 times* and rapidly rising when adjusted for recent trend).

Egypt has long had the largest Christian population of any Muslim nation. In 1952, when the Egyptian army led by Gamal Abdel Nasar overthrew King Farouk and established a militantly Islamic republic, Christians may have made up as much as 20 percent of the population. Today, Christians make up no more than 10 percent, nearly all of them members of the Coptic Orthodox Church. Part of the decline is due to Copts having a lower fertility rate than Egypt's Muslims. But part is due to the fact that Copts began immigrating over the past several decades because of increasing levels of persecution.

A major incident occurred in June 1981, when a mob of Muslims rioted and killed eighty-one Copts. Subsequently, the Egyptian government greatly increased its security forces in Coptic areas, and there was no similar incident until May 1992, when Muslims chose Easter Sunday (on the Coptic calendar) to attack a Coptic community, killing six and injuring fifty. In 1997, masked terrorists burst into a Coptic church and shot eight attending a youth group meeting. In January 2000, Muslim rioters attacked the Coptic town of el-Kosheh, killing twenty-one and destroying 260 shops. Government security forces arrested eighty-nine Muslims and charged them with murder. All were acquitted. In January 2010, as Coptic Christians were leaving church in the city of Nag Hammadi after a midnight mass celebrating Christmas Eve (Coptic calendar), Muslim terrorists machine-gunned them, killing eight and wounding nine.

But it wasn't until 2011, as growing challenges began to build up against the rule of President Hosni Mubarak, that brutal attacks on the Coptic community became chronic. It began on New Year's Eve, when a car bomb exploded in front of the Coptic Orthodox Church in Alexandria, killing twenty-three and injuring ninety-seven. President Mubarak went on television to denounce the attack as the work of "foreign elements," and no arrests ever were made. But now attacks on Copts became frequent. In March, a church was burned in the village of Sole. In April, several Copts were killed, ten were hospitalized, and many homes, shops, and businesses were looted and burned by a Muslim mob in a southern Egyptian town. In May, an anti-Coptic riot killed fifteen and injured fifty-five as a church, homes, and shops were burned. A week later there was a huge demonstration by Copts in front of the TV station in Maspero, protesting the destruction of the Coptic church in Aswan by order of the governor. The army set upon the demonstrators, crushing some by driving over them with armored vehicles, killing twenty-eight and injuring 322—about 250 of them being hospitalized.

In August 2012, the new "democratic" government headed by President Mohamed Morsi was installed. As this took place, the entire Christian community of Dahshour—about 100 families—fled from Muslim rioters who destroyed their homes and properties and torched their church. The new government took no action. And attacks on Copts accelerated under the new regime, which quickly revealed its militant Muslim character.

- *October 19, 2012*: Egyptian television carries a broadcast during which an imam prays, " Oh Allah, . . . grant us victory over the infidels. Oh Allah, destroy the Jews and their supporters." To which the new president of Egypt, Mohamed Morsi, who is present, responds, "Amen."[29]

- *April 7, 2013*: After a funeral service in Cairo for four Christians killed by Muslim militants two days earlier, mourners leaving the Coptic Orthodox Cathedral are attacked by a Muslim mob who shower them with stones and fire bombs, killing one and wounding eighty. The police take no action—some of those throwing fire bombs do so from behind police lines. As the U.S. State Department 2013 report put it before this event took place, "The government failed to protect Christians and their property effectively."[30]

- *July 3, 2013*: The government of Mohammad Morsi is overthrown by an army coup and turmoil ensues, during which some Egyptians take the opportunity to attack the Copts. The attacks quickly accelerate. Hundreds of churches are burned. Monasteries are gutted. Businesses are sacked. The death rate rises. Neither the local police nor the army does anything to prevent or punish these attacks, in part because they, too, are anti-Christian, and in part because they do not want to be discredited as allies of the Copts.

Consequently, a Coptic exodus has continued to grow. Samuel Tadros estimates that during the first eighteen months after the fall of the Mobarak regime in 2011, more than one hundred thousand Copts left Egypt.[31] Since then the number has increased, and it seems likely that many more would leave had they the means to do so and somewhere to go. and why aren't we taking them

Cleansing Allah's Domain

In the year 300 AD, far more than half of all Christians lived in the Middle East and North Africa. Then, in the seventh and early eighth century, these areas were overrun by Islam. Initially the Muslim conquerors were content to rule over indigenous Christian communities. Then, in the fourteenth century, came a relentless and violent Muslim campaign of extermination and forced conversions.

It began in Cairo in 1321, when Muslim mobs began destroying Coptic churches. These anti-Christian riots "were carefully orchestrated throughout Egypt"[32] until large numbers of churches and monasteries were destroyed. Although the mobs eventually were put down by Mamlûk authorities, small-scale anti-Christian attacks, arson, looting, and murder became chronic and widespread. Then in 1354, mobs once again "ran amok, destroying churches ... and attacking Christians and Jews in the streets, and throwing them into bonfires if they refused to pronounce the *shadâdatayn*"[33] (to acknowledge Allah as the one true God). Soon, according to Al-Maqrizi's (1364-1442) account, in "all the provinces of Egypt, both north and south, no church remained that had not been razed. ... Thus did Islam spread among the Christians of Egypt."[34] It was not a muslim country

The massacres of Christians and the destruction of churches and monasteries were not limited to Egypt. Having converted to Islam, the Mongol rulers of Mesopotamia, Armenia, and Syria took even more draconian measures than did the Mamlûks. When Ghâzân took the Mongol throne of Iran in 1295, he converted to Islam in pursuit of increased public support (he had been raised a Christian and then became a Buddhist) and yielded to "popular pressure which compelled him to ... persecute Christians."[35] According to an account written by the Nestorian patriarch Mar Yabballaha III (1245-1317), in keeping with his aim of forcing all Christians and Jews to become Muslims, Ghâzân issued this edict:

> *The churches shall be uprooted, and the altars over-turned, and the celebrations of the Eucharist shall cease, and the hymns of praise and the sounds of calls to prayer shall be abolished; and the heads of the Christians, and the heads of the congregations of the Jews, and the great men among them, shall be killed.*[36]

Within a year Ghâzân changed his mind and attempted to end the persecutions of Christians, but by now the mobs were out of control, and it was widely accepted "that everyone who did not abandon Christianity and deny his faith should be killed."[37]

Meanwhile, similar events were taking place in Mongol Armenia. In an effort to force Christians into Islam, church services were forbidden, and a crushing tax was imposed on each Christian. In addition, local authorities were ordered to seize each Christian man, pluck out his beard, and tattoo a black mark on his shoulder. When few Christians defected in response to these measures, the Khân then ordered that all Christian men be castrated and have one eye put out—which caused many deaths in this era before antibiotics but did lead to many conversions.[38]

In 1310 there was "a terrible massacre in Arbil" in Mesopotamia.[39] Things were no better in Syria. In 1317 the city of Âmid was the scene of an anti-Christian attack. The bishop was beaten to death, then churches were all burned, the Christian men were all murdered, and twelve thousand women and children were sold into slavery.[40] Similar events occurred all across the Middle East and North Africa.[41] Thus was the number of Christians in this area reduced to less than 2 percent of the population by 1400.[42]

It would seem that militant Islamic forces now are determined to finish the job, to rid their region of this last 2 percent. And what's to stop them? Indeed, nobody stopped them when, in the aftermath of World War II, militant Muslims in North Africa and the Middle East drove out all but a tiny remnant of the local Jewish populations, notwithstanding the dreadful revelations of the Nazi Holocaust—which, then as now, many leading Muslims either denied as having taken place or praised.

Jewish Exodus from Western Europe

Today, although there are very few Jews living in most Western European nations, according to Gallup World Poll findings, about a third of them would like to leave within the next year! The primary reason is the threat of anti-Semitic violence by local Islamic militants. A report issued by the U.S. Department of State sums up the situation:

> *Anti-Semitism in Europe increased significantly in recent years.... Beginning in 2000, verbal attacks directed against Jews increased, while incidents of vandalism (e.g. graffiti, fire bombings of Jewish schools, desecration of synagogues and cemeteries) surged. Physical assaults including beatings, stabbings and other violence against Jews in Europe increased markedly, in a number of cases resulting in serious injury and even death. Also troubling is the bias that spills over into anti-Semitism in some of the left-of-center press and among intellectuals.*[43]

Most of the attacks on Jews and Jewish property are by young Muslims, and the State Department noted that the threat against Jews is likely to increase since "the number of Muslims in Europe continues to grow." Even now, in all European nations Muslims greatly outnumber the Jews. While France, Great Britain, and Germany have by far the largest Jewish populations, even in these three nations, Jews are outnumbered by Muslims by more than eight to one. Elsewhere the ratios are even much higher—for example, 80/1 in Spain, 72/1 in Norway, 70/1 in Denmark, 53/1 in Italy, 28/1 in the Netherlands, and 25/1 in Sweden.

These overwhelming differences have two obvious consequences. First, Jews are hopelessly outnumbered in terms of self-defense. Second, Jews are of comparatively little political significance. Moreover, as the State Department report noted, the political left often sides with the Muslims. The city of Malmo in Sweden provides a sad example.

Malmo is a city of about three hundred thousand located at the southern tip of Sweden, connected by a bridge to Denmark. There are about forty thousand Muslims in Malmo, mostly first-generation immigrants, and there are about seven hundred Jews, many of them descendants of survivors of the Holocaust. In 2009, the synagogue was set on fire. Subsequently, the Jewish cemetery has repeatedly been vandalized, tombstones painted with swastikas, and Jews frequently mocked on the street. The synagogue now has guards and bullet-proof windows. The Jewish kindergarten can only be reached through thick security doors. The mayor explains that what the Jews regard as anti-Semitism is, in fact, the understandable consequence of Israeli policies in the Middle East. It is estimated that in the past several years, thirty Jewish families have left Malmo, some to Israel, some to Great Britain. More are planning to go. The mayor has told the press that "if Jews from the city want to move to Israel, that is not a matter for Malmo."[44] *Who is it a matter for*

Meanwhile, in the Netherlands, the Chief Rabbi has responded to the worsening situation by asserting that "the future of Dutch Jewry is moving to Israel."[45] In France, Jews have been murdered recently by Muslims, and attacks on Jews have been escalating. There is much said and written in French Jewish circles about leaving, as there is elsewhere across the continent. But there are no trustworthy statistics available. Immigration statistics for nations most often given as destinations for European Jews—the United States, Great Britain, Canada, New Zealand, and Australia—do not record religion. All we know for sure is that some Jews are leaving Europe, and a third say they would like to join them.

Chapter Eight:
True Faiths and Civility

There is nothing new about religious conflict. It is impossible even to guess how many millions have died, if not for their faith, then because of it. In Europe alone, over past centuries the death toll has run into many millions. For example, the attack on the French Cathars, known as the Albigensian Crusade (1208-1249), is thought to have killed a million,[1] many of them executed. The French Religious Wars (1562-1598), that pitted Catholics versus Protestant Huguenots, are estimated to have caused three million deaths.[2] And the Thirty Years War (1618-1648), initiated by Catholic France and Spain in hopes of destroying the Protestant movement in Germany and Scandinavia, is believed to have killed 7.5 million.[3]

[handwritten margin note: the Huguenots were the ones who died.]

[handwritten margin note: against]

Can anything be done to prevent religious conflict? The most "popular" solution on the Internet is to get rid of religion. That is about as pertinent as to propose eliminating academic failure by doing away with education. Fortunately, we are not without a model for achieving a climate of religious civility, wherein millions remain deeply committed to a variety of quite particularistic religions and do so without offending one another. Of course, it is one thing to have such a model; it is another to put it into practice.

In this final chapter, we evaluate the two leading proposed solutions for ending religious conflict by testing them against the actual American achievement of religious civility, and then we explore whether the American example can possibly be adopted elsewhere.

The Monopoly "Solution" to Religious Conflict

How can people be induced to live in harmony? Until quite recently the answer was always found in collective means of repression, usually by the state. Thomas Hobbes (1588-1679) concluded that in the absence of a powerful state, human selfishness would produce a life that was "solitary, poor, nasty, brutish, and short."[4] To prevent this dismal state of affairs, Hobbes advised that it is necessary for humans to impose "a constraint upon themselves" in the form of "some power ... contrary to their natural Passions ... the Commonwealth."[5] As for religious conflict, Hobbes advised that tranquility required the state to thwart all outbursts of religious dissent—at least until such time as humans outgrew their "credulity" and "ignorance" and rejected all Gods as merely "creatures of their own fancy,"[6] thus anticipating the current Internet solution by five centuries. Meanwhile, Hobbes continued, there must only be one authoritative church wherein the "Civil Sovereign is the Supreme Pastor, to whose charge the whole flock of his Subjects is committed, and consequently it is by his authority, that all Pastors are made, and have the power to teach, and perform all other Pastoral offices."[7] That is, if everyone must submit to the same church, there can be no opposition and therefore no conflict. a dream

David Hume (1711-1776) agreed. Social disruption and violence are inherent in religious diversity; to eliminate these evils, eliminate diversity. Where there is a religious monopoly, there can only be religious tranquility. In contrast, when there are many sects within a society, the leaders of each will express "the most violent abhorrence of all other sects," causing no end of trouble for the governing elite, and therefore wise politicians will support and sustain a single religious organization and will swiftly repress all challengers.[8]

The monopoly solution looks good on paper, the logic being impeccable. But it is historically and sociologically naive. The effort to sustain a monopoly church and to repress sectarian challenges was the primary basis for Europe's religious wars! And the attempts to impose monopolies are responsible for much of the current violence within Islam. The simple fact is that no single religious body can satisfy the diverse religious preferences that always exist in any society—be it a small, preliterate tribe or an advanced modern nation.

exactly what muslims have been trying to do

Diverse Religious Preferences

To begin, let us be clear about what religion is and what it does. Religion is best defined as an explanation of existence (or ultimate meaning) based on supernatural assumptions and including statements about the nature of the supernatural, which may specify methods or procedures for exchanging with the supernatural.[9] Use of the term *supernatural*, defined as "forces or entities (conscious or not) that are beyond or outside nature and which can suspend, alter or ignore physical forces,"[10] allows the definition to include religions having many gods as well as those with only one. It also recognizes that a primary function of all religious activities—rituals, rites, and other forms of worship—is to exchange with a god or gods. That is, people seek to obtain things from a god or gods, in exchange for various offerings or for observing certain behavioral rules.[11]

As it turns out, in every society people differ in the intensity of their religious desires and tastes. Some people want much from religion and are willing to give much to gain it. Others—usually the majority—want a less expensive religion. And some want no religion at all—"unbelievers" have been observed even in very primitive groups.[12] It turns out that because of the diversity in religious tastes, there exists a relatively stable set of demand or preference *niches*—sets of persons sharing similar religious preferences—in all societies. The distribution of the population across these niches tends to resemble a normal curve, with the majority of persons wanting a religion that places some demands upon them, but not too many. Quite similar set niches have been identified in many Western nations,[13] in Islam,[14] in China,[15] and in ancient Rome,[16] and there is no reason to assume they are not universal.

The existence of these religious niches means that *pluralism*, the existence of an array of religious groups, is the *natural* condition (although not the *usual* condition) of any society. It is the natural condition because no single religious group can satisfy the full array of niches, as no single organization can be at once highly demanding and lax, very worldly and very otherworldly. The existence of these niches need not pose a problem in polytheistic societies wherein people can pursue the god(s) of their choice as ardently or as little as they like. However, if a single religious group attempts to impose itself as the one true monopoly, by doing so it will always generate discontent ready to burst forth into bitter opposition whenever the opportunity arises. Indeed, because the repressive monopoly religion will normally reflect the moderate religious tastes of the largest niche, dissatisfaction and potential opposition will be rooted in the niche of those favoring the most intense forms of religion. This makes religious conflicts especially bitter.

Adam Smith's Pluralist Solution

So much, then, for the proposition that the solution to religious conflict is to impose a monopoly church. Rather than being the solution, it is, instead, a major part of the problem. Indeed, unlike his friend David Hume, Adam Smith was fully aware of the danger of attempts to impose religious monopolies. As he explained, religious differences "can be dangerous and troublesome only where there is either but one sect [religious body] tolerated in the society, or where the whole of a large society is divided into two or three great seets."[17] As Smith realized, the latter tends to be a very unstable situation, as one group usually attempts to wipe out the other(s), as between the Cathars and the Catholics or the Sunnis and the Shi'ah.

How then to minimize religious conflict? Smith had a creative answer. Conflict can be avoided:

> ... where the society is divided into two of three hundred, or perhaps as many [as a] thousand small sects, of which no one could be considerable enough to disturb the publick tranquility. The teachers of each sect, seeing themselves surrounded on all sides with more adversaries than friends, would be obliged to learn the candour and moderation which is so seldom to be found among the teachers of great sects ... The teachers of each little sect, finding themselves almost alone, would be obliged to respect those of almost every other sect, and the concessions which they would mutually find it both convenient and agreeable to make to one another ... [would result in] publick tranquility.[18]

That is, as each weak religious group seeks to secure itself from attack, self-interest will lead to the collective observance of civility. Put more formally: Where there exist particularistic religions, norms of religious civility will develop to the extent that the society achieves a pluralistic equilibrium. Norms of civility consist of public behavior that is governed by mutual respect among faiths, hence moderation of particularistic commitments in public expressions. A pluralistic equilibrium exists when power is sufficiently diffused among a set of religious bodies so that conflict is not in anyone's interest.

Of course, Smith was assuming that all this took place in a "free market" wherein the government did not take sides, indeed, where any government actions vis-à-vis religious groups were protective of religious liberty. Otherwise, Smith's analysis fails to anticipate coalition formation within pluralism. Indeed, at the very time Smith wrote, Protestant pluralism was sufficient in Great Britain to protect the many "dissenting" sects, but Catholics still suffered from considerable discrimination imposed by the Protestant coalition—Catholic students were excluded from Oxford and Cambridge until 1895! Similarly, real estate covenants attached to deeds excluded Jews and often Catholics from many fashionable Protestant neighborhoods in the United States until outlawed in the 1950s and 1960s. Hence, in addition to a pluralistic equilibrium, religious civility requires a neutral and libertarian state.

American Civility

Particularistic religious groups do not learn tolerance by having been persecuted. Thus, for example, although they fled persecution in England and were barely tolerated during their stay in Holland, the Puritans learned nothing about tolerance but only about their need for power. The Massachusetts Bay Colony was, from the start, committed to an utter intolerance of any religious diversity. In 1636 (only sixteen years after the landing at Plymouth Rock), the Puritans banished Roger Williams (who then founded the first Baptist church in America in Rhode Island). The next year they tried Anne Hutchison for heresy and banished her, along with her fifteen children—she resettled in the Dutch colony of New Amsterdam. Whenever Quakers were detected, even if they were merely in transit aboard a ship in Boston Harbor, they were subjected to public whippings before being expelled from the colony. Between 1659 and 1661, four Quakers who had been whipped and driven out of Massachusetts were hanged for having returned. Tolerance of other Protestants developed only slowly, forced by the rapid growth of Methodists and Baptists and the splitting off from the Puritan's Congregational Church by the Unitarians in 1825.

Even then, New England toleration did not extend beyond the boundaries of Protestantism. In 1834, Lyman Beecher, the most prominent Congregationalist preacher of the day (and whose daughter wrote the antislavery classic *Uncle Tom's Cabin*), gave three thunderous sermons in Boston warning against the evils of Rome and of a plot by the pope to seize the Mississippi Valley. The result was an anti-Catholic riot during which a convent for Ursuline nuns was burned down. Things were much the same elsewhere in nineteenth-century America. Ten years after the Boston riot, a three-day anti-Catholic riot broke out in Philadelphia during which the city's two largest Catholic churches were torched. As for Jews, they were still too few to attract attention, but the Mormons were forced to flee to the remote Utah Territory after founder Joseph Smith and his brother Hyrum were murdered by an Illinois mob in 1844.

The first evidence of American religious civility appeared in New York City at the start of the twentieth century. This was facilitated by the fact that New York City was the most religiously diverse place in the nation, with Jews and Catholics each making up about a quarter of the population. The pivotal occasion occurred in 1904 at St. Mark's Evangelical Lutheran Church in Manhattan, following the tragic drowning of more than a thousand of St. Mark's Sunday school students, teachers, and choir members when their tour boat caught fire and sank several miles off shore in New York Harbor. During the huge memorial service held at St. Mark's, a message was read from the Catholic archbishop of New York: "May the Giver of all strength comfort you and yours in this dreadful hour of your sorrow." And at the end of the service, several hundred Lutheran, Methodist, Episcopal, and Presbyterian clergy joined with a number of Jewish rabbis to sing (in German), "Who Knows How Near My End May Be?"[19]

Note that the archbishop referred to the "Giver of all strength," rather than to Almighty God or to Jesus Christ. This was a model expression of religious civility, which is to not fully say what one truly believes, but to modify one's remarks out of deference to what others present truly believe. Sociologists often refer to such expressions as instances of civil religion.

Civil religion consists of expressions of religion to which everyone (or nearly everyone) making up the public can assent. It is particularly on display during civic occasions such as Memorial Day observances or other public ceremonies such as the singing of "God Bless America" during the seventh inning of baseball games—that grand anthem having been written by a Jew who was married to a Catholic.

It should be recognized that, being constrained by the norms of civility, the civil religion is not the actual religion of *anyone*. It holds the power to move people because it triggers a response in each individual based on her or his far more vital and distinctive faith. Put another way, different people hear quite different things when the civil religion is invoked, depending on their personal religious convictions. And that's why it works.

By the 1960s, religious Americans had achieved civility among an extensive diversity of faiths. Interfaith organizations and conferences have become commonplace. Indeed, research shows that the more religious they are, the more favorable Americans are toward other religious groups.[20] But incivility persists between the religious and the antireligious, with even the civil religion having become a battleground—although the antagonism tends to be one-sided, with the irreligious being more actively hostile.

Unfortunately, in this dispute the tiny portion of antireligious Americans enjoy a very significant advantage—the news media are on their side! They relish exposing religious "fanatics" who are angry about the use of government funds to display virulently antireligious art such as Serrano's *Piss Christ*, consisting of a crucifix in a tube of urine. Five people demonstrating outside a Catholic church on behalf of the ordination of female priests can expect sympathetic coverage; one thousand people holding a vigil outside an abortion clinic cannot. Indeed, the media gladly give favorable coverage to the secularist's campaign even against the civil religion. No religious expression is completely inclusive, all of it being an affront to the nonbelievers. Therefore, it is argued, all public expressions of religion should be suppressed—no prayers of any sort, no matter how inter-religious, should ever be uttered at public events—and all "religious" holidays should be sanitized into full secularity: "Jingle Bells," maybe; "Silent Night," never. Consequently, many under the age of forty do not know the words to either song! That this is an affront to the majority ✳ seems to count for nothing.

Global Prospects

Nevertheless, civility prevails among American religions. But is it exportable? We think not. The reason is that the aphorism that "all politics is local" is especially true at the international level. Just as Americans did not import religious civility but developed it through many years of trial and error, other nations probably will have to do the same.

In that regard, America may have had a unique situation favoring the development of religious civility. The Founding Fathers might not have opted for religious freedom had there existed one dominant religious body suitable to be established as the state church. But in 1776, although the Puritan Congregationalists were the largest denomination, they made up only 20 percent of the nation's congregations, and they had only a dozen or so congregations outside of New England. All told, there were seventeen different religious bodies holding regular services in colonial America.[21] Since then, American religious diversity has expanded greatly. Today there are hundreds of Protestant denominations—twenty-five of them have more than a million members each. In addition, Catholics make up about a quarter of Americans, joined by millions of Jews (more ✳ than in Israel), as well as millions of Mormons and substantial numbers of Buddhists, Muslims, and Hindus.

This sort of diversity exists nowhere else. Neither does the American level of religious civility—recall from Chapter 6 how much discrimination, even against many Christian groups, there is in Europe. Consider, too, that during the two nineteenth-century anti-Catholic riots in Boston and Philadelphia ✳reported above, not one Catholic was killed! If only that were the case in much of the world today.

Nevertheless, here stands the American example, giving the lie to any claims that an end to religious hostility is impossible. *But muslims are trying to end it.*

Endnotes

Introduction

[1] First in 1992 in a lecture at the American Enterprise Institute. Then, fully developed, in his 1996 book. Samuel Huntington, *The Clash of Civilizations: Remaking the World Order* (New York: Simon & Schuster).

[2] Stuart A. Wright, *Armageddon in Waco* (Chicago: University of Chicago Press, 1995).

[3] Jess Walter, *The Truth and Tragedy of the Randy Weaver Family* (New York: Harpers, 2002).

Chapter One

[1] The very best of these are assembled by David Barrett and his associ-ates.

[2] Rodney Stark and Eric Y. Liu, "The Religious Awakening in China," *Review of Religious Research*. 52(2011):282-289.

[3] Rodney Stark, Carson Mencken, and Byron Johnson, "A Reliable Estimate of the Number of Chinese Christians."*First Things*. May(2011), 14-16.

[4] Ibid.

[5] Stark and Liu, "The Religious Awakening in China."

[6] See: Mark A. Noll, *The New Shape of World Christianity: How American Experience Reflects Global Faith* (Downers Grove: InterVarsity Press, 2009), 22.

[7] Huntington, *The Clash of Civilizations*.

[8] Phillip Jenkins, *The Next Christendom: The Rise of Global Christianity* (New York: Oxford University Press, 2002).

[9] Tomas Frejka and Charles F. Westoff, "Religion, Religiousness and Fertil-ity in the US and in Europe." *European Journal of Population* 24 (2008):5-31; Eric Kaufmann, *Shall the Religious Inherit the Earth?*(London: Profile Books, 2010).

[10] Kaufmann, *Shall the Religious Inherit the Earth?*; Rodney Stark, *America's Blessings: How Religion Benefits Everyone Including Atheists* (Conshohoken, PA: Templeton Foundation Press, 2012).

Chapter Two

[1] Of particular value are those gathered by *thereligionofpeace.com*, the list of terrorist incidents assembled by Wikipedia, and the Political Instability Task Force Worldwide Atrocities Data Set, Philip A. Schrodt, director. We also consulted the annual report on worldwide anti-Semitic incidents issue by Tel Aviv University. The United States Commission on International

Religious Freedom's annual report for 2013 was also useful, as was the U.S. State Department's *International Freedom Report*, 2013.

2 Mark Juergensmeyer, *Terror in the Mind of God*. 3rd edition. (Berkeley: University of California Press, 2003).

3 Jess Walter, *The Truth and Tragedy of the Randy Weaver Family*.

4 See the excellent article on "Boko Haram" in Wikipedia.

5 Data come from the Pew Forum on Religion & Public Life's April 2013 report: *The World's Muslims: Religion, Politics, and Society* and from the Sub-Saharan Africa Survey, 2010. Respondents who answered 'don't know" or who refused to answer were left in the calculations. The Pew Research Center bears no responsibility for the analyses or interpretations of the data presented here. The Sub-Saharan Africa data was downloaded from the Association of Religious Data Archives, www. TheARDA.com.

6 Mark Juergensmeyer, "Don't Blame Religion for Boston Bombings." *Religion Dispatches.org*, April 22, 2013.

7 In *The Nation*, September 11, 2002.

8 See the excellent summary in "Islamophobia," Wikipedia.

9 May 28, 2013: A15.

10 Quoted in Ayaan Hirsi Ali, "The Problem of Muslim Leadership," *The Wall Street Journal*, May 27, 2013.

11 Stark, *God's Battalions: The Case for the Crusades* (San Francisco: HarperOne, 2009).

Chapter Three

1 For a summary see Gertrude J. Selznick and Stephen Steinberg, *The Tenacity of Prejudice: Anti-Semitism in Contemporary America* (New York: Harper and Row, 1969).

2 Charles Y. Glock and Rodney Stark, *Christian Beliefs and Anti-Semitism* (New York: Harper and Row, 1966).

3 Tom W. Smith, "The Religious Right and Anti-Semitism," *Review of Religious Research* 40, 3(1999):244-258.

4 Johnson, 1984.

5 Arnold Forster and Benjamin R. Epstein, *The New Anti-Semitism* (New York: McGraw-Hill, 1974).

6 Richard Kerbaj, "MPs condemn hate sermons on Arabic TV station al-Jazeera," *The Times*, February 7, 2009.

7 Fox News, October 16, 2003.

8 Middle East Media Research Institute, special dispatch 2278, March 12, 2009.

9 *Saudi Arabia's Curriculum of Intolerance*. Freedom House. May 2006:24-25.

10 Leon Watson, "The Arabic school textbooks which show children how to chop off hands and feet under Sharia law," *The Daily Mail*, December 23, 2011.

11 The data were downloaded from the Association of Religion Data Archives, www.TheARDA.com, and were collected by the International Social Survey Programme Research Group.

[12] Data come from the Religion and Public Life Survey, 2009 and were collected by the Pew Forum on Religion & Public Life (a project of The Pew Research Center). The Pew Research Center bears no responsibility for the analyses or interpretations of the data presented here. The data were downloaded from the Association of Religion Data Archives, www.TheARDA.com.

[13] Freedom House, 2005:11.

[14] Freedom House, 2005:28.

[15] Freedom House, 2005:21.

[16] Freedom House, 2005:39.

[17] The data were downloaded from the Association of Religion Data Archives, www.TheARDA.com, and were collected by the International Social Survey Programme Research Group.

[18] Data come from the Global Attitudes Survey, 2008 and were collected by the Pew Research Global Attitudes Project. The Pew Research Center bears no responsibility for the analyses or interpretations of the data presented here.

[19] The data were downloaded from the Association of Religion Data Archives, www.TheARDA.com, and were collected by the International Social Survey Programme Research Group.

[20] Data come from the Global Attitudes Survey, 2008 and were collected by the Pew Research Global Attitudes Project. The Pew Research Center bears no responsibility for the analyses or interpretations of the data presented here.

[21] Data come from the Religion and Public Life Survey, 2009 and were collected by the Pew Forum on Religion & Public Life (a project of The Pew Research Center). The Pew Research Center bears no responsibility for the analyses or interpretations of the data presented here. The data were downloaded from the Association of Religion Data Archives, www.TheARDA.com

[22] Data come from the Muslim American Survey, 2007 and were collected by the Pew Forum on Religion & Public Life (a project of The Pew Research Center) and the Pew Research Center for the People & the Press. The Pew Research Center bears no responsibility for the analyses or interpretations of the data presented here.

[23] Glock and Stark, *Christian Beliefs and Anti-Semitism.*

[24] Shaye J. D. Cohen, *From the Maccabees to the Mishnah* (Philadelphia: Westminster Press, 1987); Dieter Georgi, "The Early Church: Internal Migration of New Religion," *Harvard Theological Review* 88(1995):35-68.

[25] Michael Allen Williams, *Rethinking "Gnosticism": An Argument for Dismantling a Dubious Category* (Princeton, Princeton University Press, 1996).

[26] Rodney Stark, "A Theory of Revelations," *Journal for the Scientific Study of Religion* 38,2(1999a):287-308.

[27] Gregory Baum, ed. *The Teachings of the Second Vatican Council: Complete Texts of the Constitutions, Decrees, and Declarations* (Westminster: The Newman Press,1966),184.

[28] Pew Forum on Religion and Public Life, *The World's Muslims: Religion Politics and Society*. (Washington, DC, 2013).

[29] Ibid, Appendix A:140.

[30] Ibid,112.

Chapter Four

[1] In Albert Henry Newman, *A History of the Baptist Churches in the United States*, 6th ed (New York: Charles Scribner's Sons, 1915), 519.

[2] Anthony F.C.Wallace, *Religion: An Anthropological View* (New York: Random House,1966), 264-265.

[3] Peter Berger, "A Bleak Outlook is Seen for Religion,"*New York Times*, April 25, 1968, 3.

[4] Ariela Keysar, Egon Mayer, and Barry A. Kosmin, "No Religion: A Profile of America's Unchurched," *Public Perspective* 14 (2003):28-32.

[5] Rodney Stark, *Exploring the Religious Life* (Baltimore: Johns Hopkins University Press, 2004), Ch. 6.

[6] James R. Kluegel, "Denominational Mobility," *Journal for the Scientific Study of Religion* 19(1980):26-39 and Darren E. Sherkat and John Wilson, "Preferences, Constraints, and Choices in Religious Markets," *Social Forces* 73(1995):993-1026.

[7] University of California Press, 2008.

[8] January 11, 2007.

[9] October, 2006.

[10]"Remembering the Secular Age," *First Things*, June/July, 2007.

[11] Richard Cimino and Christopher Smith, "Secular Humanism and Atheism Beyond Progressive Secularism." *Sociology of Religion* 68(2007):407-424.

[12] Rodney Stark, *What Americans Really Believe* (Waco: Baylor University Press, 2008), Ch.20.

[13] Gary A. Tobin and Aryeh K. Weinberg, *Profiles of the American University: Religious Beliefs and Behavior of College Faculty* (San Francisco: Institute for Jewish & Community Studies, 2007).

[14] Data come from the *Religion and Public Life Survey*, 2009 and were collected by the Pew Forum on Religion & Public Life (a project of The Pew Research Center). The Pew Research Center bears no responsibility for the analyses or interpretations of the data presented here. The data were downloaded from the Association of Religion Data Archives, www.TheARDA.com.

[15] Kevin Phillips, *American Theocracy: The Peril and Politics of Radical Religion, Oil, and Borrowed Money in the 21st Century* (New York: Penguin Group, 2007).

[16] Sam Harris, *Letter to a Christian Nation* (New York: Random House, 2006).

[17] Paul Blanshard, *American Freedom and Catholic Power* (Boston: Beacon Press, [1949] 1958), 346.

[18] Robert L. Rafford, "Atheophobia: An Introduction."*Religious Humanism* 21(1987):33.

[19] The data were downloaded from the Association of Religion Data Archives, www.TheARDA.com, and were collected by the International Social Survey Programme Research Group.

[20] Data come from the Religion and Public Life Surveys and were collected by the Pew Forum on Religion & Public Life (a project of The Pew Research Center). The Pew Research Center bears no responsibility for the analyses or interpretations of the data presented here. The data were downloaded from the Association of Religion Data Archives, www.TheARDA.com.

Chapter Five

[1] Respondents were presented with a scale from 1 through 5, with 1 being "Not justified" and 5 being "Completely justified." We have merged 4 and 5 to equal "Justified."

[2] Data come from the Pew Forum on Religion & Public Life's April 2013 report on *The World's Muslims: Religion, Politics and Society*, < http://www.pewforum.org/Muslim/the-worlds-muslims-religion-politics-society.aspx>. Respondents who answered with "Don't know" or refused to answer were left in the sample. The Pew Research Center bears no responsibility for the analyses or interpretations of the data presented here.

[3] Data come from the Pew Forum on Religion & Public Life's April 2013 report on *The World's Muslims: Religion, Politics and Society*, < http://www.pewforum.org/Muslim/the-worlds-muslims-religion-politics-society.aspx>. Respondents who answered with "Don't know" or refused to answer were left in the sample. The Pew Research Center bears no responsibility for the analyses or interpretations of the data presented here.

[4] Pew Forum on Religion & Public Life, a project of the Pew Research Center. 2013. *Arab Spring Adds to Global Restrictions on Religion*. <http://www.pewforum.org/Government/arab-spring-restrictions-on-religion.aspx>.

[5] Phyllis Chesler, "Are Honor Killings Simply Domestic Violence?" *Middle East Quarterly* (2009):61-69.

[6] Phyllis Chesler, and Yotam Feldner, "'Honor' Murders—Why the Perps Get off Easy," *Middle East Quarterly* (2000):41-50.

[7] Data come from the Pew Forum on Religion & Public Life's April 2013 report on *The World's Muslims: Religion, Politics and Society*, < http://www.pewforum.org/Muslim/the-worlds-muslims-religion-politics-society.aspx>. Respondents who answered with "Don't know" or refused to answer were left in the sample. The Pew Research Center bears no responsibility for the analyses or interpretations of the data presented here.

[8] *State of Human Rights in Pakistan in 2012*. Islamabad, Pakistan, May 4, 2013.

[9] Tarif Khalidi, "The Idea of Progress," *Journal of Near Eastern Studies* 40(October 1981):279.

[10] Data come from the Global Attitudes Survey, 2008 and were collected by the Pew Research Global Attitudes Project. The Pew Research Center

bears no responsibility for the analyses or interpretations of the data presented here.

[11]Marc Sageman, *Understanding Terror Networks* (Philadelphia: University of Pennsylvania Press, 2004); Lawrence Wright, *The Looming Tower* (New York: Vintage Press 2007).

Chapter 6

[1] U.S. State Department, 2013: "Saudi Arabia."

[2] U.S. State Department, 2013: "Saudi Arabia."

[3] In Paul Marshall, Lela Gilbert, and Nina Shea. *Persecuted: The Global Assault on Christians* (Nashville: Thomas Nelson, 2013), 158.

[4] U.S. State Department, 2013: "Saudi Arabia."

[5] Marshall, Gilbert, and Shea. *Persecuted*, 156.

[6] Ibid, 52.

[7] Ibid, 1; U.S. State Department, 2013: "Korea, Democratic People's Republic of."

[8] Grim and Finke, "International Religion Indexes: Government Regulation, Government Favoritism, and Social Regulation of Religion," *Interdisciplinary Journal of Research on Religion* 2,1 (2006):1-40

[9] Grim and Finke chose to call it government regulation of religion.

[10] Peter Berger, Grace Davie, and Effie Fokas, *Religious America, Secular Europe?:A Theme and Variation* (Burlington: Ashgate Publishing Company, 2008),16.

[11] Gerhard Schmied, "American Televangelism on German TV," *Journal of Contemporary Religion* 11, 1(1996):95-99.

[12]James A. Beckford, *Cult Controversies: The societal response to new religious movements* (London: Tavistock Publications, 1985), 286.

[13]Peter Lodberg, "The Churches in Denmark," in Danish Christian Handbook , ed. Peter Brierly (London: MARC Europe, 1989).

[14]Steve Selthoffer, "German charismatic churches face persecution, threats of violence," *Charisma* November(1995):18-20; Steve Selthoffer, "German Government Harasses Charismatic Christians," *Charisma* June(1997):22-24.

[15]Grim and Finke, "International Religion Indexes."

[16]Ibid, 8.

[17]U.S. State Department, 2013: "Cambodia."

Chapter 7

[1] Raymond Ibrahim, *Crucified Again: Exposing Islam's New War on Christians.* (Washington, DC: Regnery, 2013a); Marshall, Gilbert, and Shea, *Persecuted*.

[2] See our colleague Thomas Kidd's fine column on this matter in *World Magazine*, June 29, 2013:86.

[3] Thomas Schirrmacher, "A Response to the High Counts of Christian Martyrs per Year," in *Sorrow and Blood: Christian Mission in the Contexts of Suffering, Persecution, and Martyrdom*, ed. William D. Taylor, Antonia van der Meer, and Reg Reimer (Pasadena: William Carey Library, 2012), 39.

[4] Quoted in Raymond Ibrahim, "The Mass Exodus of Christians from the Muslim World." *FoxNews.com,* May 7.2013b.

[5] Daniel Brode, Roger Farhat, and Daniel Nisman, "Syria's Threatened Christians." *New York Times,* June 28, 2012.

[6] *Faith on the Move,* 2012.

[7] Marshall, Gilbert, and Shea, *Persecuted,*173.

[8] U.S. State Department, 2013: "Turkey."

[9] Marshall, Gilbert, and Shea, *Persecuted,*139-140.

[10] U.S. State Department, 2013: "Iraq."

[11] Ibrahim, *Crucified Again,* 52.

[12] U.S. State Department, 2013: "India."

[13] all from Marshall, Gilbert, and Shea, *Persecuted,*98-99.

[14] "Indian Americans." *Wikipedia.*

[15] Stark, Mencken, and Johnson,, "A Reliable Estimate of the Number of Chinese Christians."

[16] Anna Xiao Dong Sun, "The fate of Confucianism as a religion in socialist China: Controversies and paradoxes," in *State, Market and Religions in Chinese Societies* eds. Fenggang Yang and Joseph B. Tamney (Leiden: Brill, 2005), 229-51.

[17] U.S. State Department, 2013:Executive Summary, p. 3.

[18] Marshall, Gilbert, and Shea, *Persecuted,*37.

[19] Ibid, 265.

[20] U.S. State Department, 2013: "Burma."

[21] U.S. State Department, 2013: "Thailand."

[22] U.S. State Department, 2013: "Thailand."

[23] U.S. State Department, 2013: "Jordan."

[24] Ninette Kelley, "Lebanon, Overrun by Syrian Refugees," *New York Times* June 19, 2013.

[25] U.S. State Department, 2013: "Libya."

[26] Maggie Michael, "Christians Say They Were Tortured in Libya," *Associated Press* March 15, 2013.

[27] U.S. State Department, 2013: "Libya."

[28] U.S. State Department, 2013: "Malaysia."

[29] U.S. State Department, 2013: "Egypt."

[30] U.S. State Department, 2013: "Egypt."

[31] Samuel Tadros, *Motherland Lost* (Stanford, CA: Hoover Institution, 2013).

[32] Donald P. Little, "Coptic Conversion to Islam under the Bahri Mamluks, 692-755/1293-1354," Bulletin of the School of Oriental and African Studies 39, 3(1976):563.

[33] Ibid, 567.

[34] Ibid, 568.

[35] Laurence Edward Browne, *The Eclipse of Christianity in Asia* (New York: Howard Fertig, [1933] 1967),163.

[36]In Richard Foltz, *Religions of the Silk Road* (New York: St. Martin's, 2000),129.

[37]Browne, *The Eclipse of Christian in Asia*, 167.

[38]Ibid, 169.

[39]Ibid, 170.

[40]Ibid, 171.

[41]Phillip Jenkins, *The Lost History of Christianity: The Thousand-Year Golden Age of the Church in the Middle East, Africa, and Asia—and How it Died* (San Francisco: HarperOne, 2008).

[42]Our calculation based on David B. Barrett, *World Christian Encyclopedia* (Oxford: Oxford University Press, 1982), 796.

[43]*Report on Global Anti-Semitism*, January 5, 2005:1

[44] "Jews Leave Swedish City After Sharp Rise in Anti-Semitic Hate Crimes," Telegraph Media Group, Ltd. February 21, 2010.

[45]"Interview With Holland's Chief Rabbi." Israel National News, July 4, 2010.

Chapter 8

[1] Christopher Brookmyre, *Not the End of the World* (New York: Grove Press, 1998), 39; Max Dimont, *Jews, God, and History* (New York: Penguin, 1994), 225

[2] Robert J. Knecht, *The French Religious Wars 1562-1598* (Oxford: Osprey Publishing, 2002).

[3] Norman Davies, *Europe: A History* (Oxford: Oxford University Press, 1996),568; Alan MacFarlane, *The Savage Wars of Peace: England, Japan, and the Malthusian Trap* (New York: Palgrave Macmillan, 2003).

[4] Thomas Hobbes, *Leviathan* (Harmondsworth: Penguin, [1651] 1968),186.

[5] Ibid, 223.

[6] Ibid, 167-168.

[7] Ibid, 569.

[8] David Hume, *The History of England* V.3 (London: A Millar, [1754] 1962):30

[9] Rodney Stark, *For the Glory of God: How Monotheism led to Reformations, Science, Witch-Hunts, and the End of Slavery* (Princeton: Princeton University Press, 2003).

[10] Stark, *For the Glory of God*, 4.

[11] Rodney Stark, "Micro Foundations of Religion: A Revised Theory", *Sociological Theory* 17, 3(1999b):264-289; Rodney Stark and Roger Finke, *Acts of Faith: Explaining the Human Side of Religion* (Berkeley: University of California Press, 2000).

[12] Mary Douglas, "The Effects of Modernization on Religious Change," in *Religion and America: Spirituality in a Secular Age*, ed. Mary Douglas and Steve M. Tipton (Boston: Beacon Press, 1982); Clifford Geertz, "Religion as a Cultural System," in *Anthropological Approaches to the Study of Religion*, ed. Michael Banton (London: Tavistock Publications, 1966).

[13] Christopher Bader and Paul Froese, "Images of God: The Effect of Personal Theologies on Moral Attitudes, Political Affiliation, and Religious Behavior," *Interdisciplinary Journal of Research on Religion* 1, 11(2005):1-24.

[14] Massimo Introvigne, "Religious Competition and Revival in Italy: Exploring European Exceptionalism," *Interdisciplinary Journal of Research on Religion* 1, 5(2005):1-20.

[15] Graeme Lang, Selina Ching Chan, and Lars Ragvald, "Folk Temples and the Chinese Religious Economy," *Interdisciplinary Journal of Research on Religion* 1, 4(2005):1-29.

[16] Mary Beard, John North, and Simon Price, *Religions of Rome: Volume 1: A History* (New York: Cambridge University Press, 1998).

[17] Adam Smith, *An Inquiry into the Nature and Causes of the Wealth of Nations* 2 vols (Indianapolis: Liberty Fund, [1776] 1981), 792-793.

[18] Ibid , 793-794.

[19] William Sims Bainbridge, *The Sociology of Religious Movements* (New York: Routledge, 1997).

[20] Smith, "The Religious Right and Anti-Semitism."

[21] Roger Finke and Rodney Stark, *The Churching of America, 1776-1990: Winners and Losers in Our Religious Economy* (New Brunswick: Rutgers University Press, 1992).

Bibliography

Ali, Ayaan Hirsi. 2013. "The Problem of Muslim Leadership," *The Wall Street Journal*, May 27.

Armstrong, Karen. 1992. *Muhammad: A Biography of a Prophet*. San Francisco: HarperSanFrancisco.

Bader, Christopher and Paul Froese. 2005. "Images of God: The Effect of Personal Theologies on Moral Attitudes, Political Affiliation, and Religious Behavior," *Interdisciplinary Journal of Research on Religion* 1(11):1-24.

Bainbridge, William Sims. 1997. *The Sociology of Religious Movements*. New York: Routledge.

Barrett, David B. 1982. *World Christian Encyclopedia*. Oxford: Oxford University Press.

Baum, Gregory. (ed.) 1966. *The Teachings of the Second Vatican Council: Complete Texts of the Constitutions, Decrees, and Declarations*. Westminster: The Newman Press.

Beard, Mary, John North, and Simon Price. 1998. *Religions of Rome: Volume 1: A History*. New York: Cambridge University Press.

Beckford, James A. 1985 *Cult Controversies: The societal response to new religious movements*. London: Tavistock Publications.

Berger, Peter. 1968. "A Bleak Outlook Is Seen for Religion," *New York Times*, April 25:3.

Berger, Peter, Grace Davie, and Effie Fokas. 2008. *Religious America, Secular Europe?:A Theme and Variation*. Burlington: Ashgate Publishing Company.

Blanshard, Paul. [1949] 1958. *American Freedom and Catholic Power*. Boston: Beacon Press.

Brode, Daniel, Roger Farhat, and Daniel Nisman. 2012. "Syria's Threatened Christians." *New York Times*, June 28.

Brookmyre, Christopher. 1998. *Not the End of the World*. New York: Grove Press.

Browne, Laurence Edward. [1933] 1967. *The Eclipse of Christianity in Asia* (New York: Howard Fertig).

Chesler, Phyllis. 2009. "Are Honor Killings Simply Domestic Violence?" *Middle East Quarterly* XVI(2): 61-69.

Chesler, Phyllis. and Yotam Feldner. 2000. "'Honor' Murders—Why the Perps Get off Easy," *Middle East Quarterly* VII(4):41-50.

Cimino, Richard and Christopher Smith. 2007. "Secular Humanism and Atheism Beyond Progressive Secularism." *Sociology of Religion* 68:407-424.

Cohen, Shaye J. D. 1987. *From the Maccabees to the Mishnah.* Philadelphia: Westminster Press.

Davies, Norman. 1996. *Europe: A History.* Oxford: Oxford University Press.

Dimont, Max. 1994. *Jews, God, and History.* New York: Penguin.

Douglas, Mary. 1982. "The Effects of Modernization on Religious Change." In *Religion and America: Spirituality in a Secular Age*, edited by Mary Douglas and Steve M. Tipton. Boston: Beacon Press.

Finke, Roger and Rodney Stark. 1992. *The Churching of America, 1776-1990: Winners and Losers in Our Religious Economy.* New Brunswick: Rutgers University Press.

Foltz, Richard. 2000. *Religions of the Silk Road.* New York: St. Martin's.

Forster, Arnold and Benjamin R. Epstein. 1974. *The New Anti-Semitism.* New York: McGraw-Hill.

Frejka, Tomas and Charles F. Westoff. 2008. "Religion, Religiousness and Fertility in the US and in Europe." *European Journal of Population* 24:5-31.

Froese, Paul. 2008. *The Plot to Kill God: Findings From the Soviet Experiment in Secularization.* Berkeley: University of California Press.

Geertz, Clifford. 1966. "Religion as a Cultural System." In *Anthropological Approaches to the Study of Religion*, edited by Michael Banton. London: Tavistock Publications.

Georgi, Dieter. 1995. "The Early Church: Internal Migration of New Religion," *Harvard Theological Review* 88:35-68.

Glock, Charles Y. and Rodney Stark. 1966. *Christian Beliefs and Anti-Semitism.* New York: Harper and Row.

Grim, Brian J. and Roger Finke. 2011. *The Price of Freedom Denied.* New York: Cambridge University Press.

_____. 2006. "International Religion Indexes: Government Regulation, Government Favoritism, and Social Regulation of Religion," *Interdisciplinary Journal of Research on Religion* 2(1):1-40

Harris, Sam. 2006. *Letter to a Christian Nation.* New York: Random House.

Hobbes, Thomas. [1651] 1968. *Leviathan.* Harmondsworth: Penguin.

Hodgson, Marshall G.S. 1974. *The Venture of Islam.* 3 vols. Chicago: University of Chicago Press.

Hume, David. [1754] 1962. *The History of Englan*d.V.3. London: A Millar.

Huntington, Samuel P. 1996. *The Clash of Civilizations: Remaking the World Order.* New York: Simon & Schuster.

Ibraham, Raymond. 2013a. *Crucified Again: Exposing Islam's New War on Christians.* Washington, DC: Regnery.

_____2013b. "The Mass Exodus of Christians from the Muslim World." *FoxNews.com,* May 7.

Introvigne, Massimo. 2005. "Religious Competition and Revival in Italy: Exploring European Exceptionalism," *Interdisciplinary Journal of Research on Religion* 1(5):1-20.

Jenkins, Phillip. 2008. *The Lost History of Christianity: The Thousand-Year Golden Age of the Church in the Middle East, Africa, and Asia—and How it Died.* San Francisco: HarperOne.

_____2002. *The Next Christendom: The Rise of Global Christianity.* New York: Oxford University Press.

Juergensmeyer, Mark. 2013. "Don't Blame Religion for Boston Bombings." *Religion Dispatches.org,* April 22.

_____2003. *Terror in the Mind of God.* 3rd edition. Berkeley: University of California Press.

Kaufmann, Eric. 2010. *Shall the Religious Inherit the Earth?* London: Profile Books.

Kelley, Ninette. 2013. "Lebanon, Overrun by Syrian Refugees." *New York Times,* June 19.

Kerbaj, Richard. 2009. "MPs condemn hate sermons on Arabic TV station al-Jazeera." *The Times,* February 7.

Keysar, Ariela, Egon Mayer, and Barry A. Kosmin. 2003. "No Religion: A Profile of America's Unchurched," *Public Perspective* 14:28-32.

Khalidi, Tarif. 1981."The Idea of Progress," *Journal of Near Easter Studies* 40:279.

Kister, M.J. 1986. "The Massacre of the Banu Qurayza: A Re-Examination of a Tradition." *Jerusalem Studies of Arabic and Islam* 8:61-96.

Kluegel, James R. 1980. "Denominational Mobility," *Journal for the Scientific Study of Religion* 19:26-39.

Knecht, Robert J. 2002. *The French Religious Wars 1562-1598.* Oxford: Osprey Publishing.

Lang, Graeme, Selina Ching Chan, and Lars Ragvald. 2005. "Folk Temples and the Chinese Religious Economy," *Interdisciplinary Journal of Research on Religion* 1(4):1-29.

Little, Donald P. 1976."Coptic Conversion to Islam under the Bahri Mamluks, 692-755/1293-1354," *Bulletin of the School of Oriental and African Studies* 39(3): 552-569

Lodberg, Peter. 1989. "The Churches in Denmark," in *Danish Christian Handbook* edited by Peter Brierly. London: MARC Europe.

Marshall, Paul, Lela Gilbert, and Nina Shea. 2013. *Persecuted: The Global Assault on Christians.* Nashville: Thomas Nelson.

Michael, Maggie. 2013. "Christians Say They Were Tortured in Libya." *Associated Press,* March 15.

Newman, Albert Henry. 1915. *A History of the Baptist Churches in the United States*, 6th ed. New York: Charles Scribner's Sons.

Noll, Mark A. 2009. *The New Shape of World Christianity: How American Experience Reflects Global Faith.* Downers Grove: InterVarsity Press.

Novak, Michael. 2007. "Remembering the Secular Age," *First Things,* June/July,

Pew Forum on Religion and Public Life. 2013. *The World's Muslims: Religion Politics and Society.* Washington, DC.

Pew Forum on Religion & Public Life. 2013. *Arab Spring Adds to Global Restrictions on Religion.* Washingto, DC.

Phillips, Kevin. 2007. *American Theocracy: The Peril and Politics of Radical Religion, Oil, and Borrowed Money in the 21st Century.* New York: Penguin Group.

Rafford, Robert L. 1987. "Atheophobia: An Introduction." *Religious Humanism* 21:33.

Rodinson, Maxime. 1980. *Muhammad*. New York: Random House.

Sageman, Marc. 2004. *Understanding Terror Networks*. Philadelphia: University of Pennsylvania Press.

Salahi, M.A. 1995. *Muhammad: Man and Prophet*. Shaftesbury, Doreset, U.K.: Element.

Schirrmacher, Thomas. 2012. "A Response to the High Counts of Christian Martyrs per Year." in Taylor, William D., Antonia van der Meer, and Reg Reimer, eds. *Sorrow and Blood: Christian Mission in the Contexts of Suffering, Persecution, and Martyrdom*. Pasadena, CA: William Carey Library.

Schmied, Gerhard. 1996. "American Televangelism on German TV." *Journal of Contemporary Religion* 11(1):95-99.

Selthoffer, Steve. 1997. "German Government Harasses Charismatic Christians," *Charisma* (June):22-24.

_____1995. "German charismatic churches face persecution, threats of violence," *Charisma* (November):18-20.

Selznick, Gertrude J. and Stephen Steinberg. 1969. *The Tenacity of Prejudice: Anti-Semitism in Contemporary America*. New York: Harper and Row.

Sherkat, Darren E. and John Wilson. 1995. "Preferences, Constraints, and Choices in Religious Markets," *Social Forces* 73:993-1026.

Smith, Adam. [1776] 1981, *An Inquiry into the Nature and Causes of the Wealth of Nations* 2 vols. Indianapolis: Liberty Fund.

Smith, Tom W. 1999. "The Religious Right and Anti-Semitism." *Review of Religious Research* 40(3):244-258.

Stark, Rodney. 2012. *America's Blessings: How Religion Benefits Everyone Including Atheists*. Conshohoken, PA: Templeton Foundation Press.

_____ and Eric Y. Liu. 2011. "The Religious Awakening in China," *Review of Religious Research*. 52:282-289.

_____, Carson Mencken, and Byron Johnson. 2011. "A Reliable Estimate of the Number of Chinese Christians." *First Things*. May, 14-16.

_____2009. *God's Battalions: The Case for the Crusades*. San Francisco: HarperOne.

_____2008. *What Americans Really Believe*. Waco: Baylor University Press.

_____2007. *Discovering God: The Origins of the Great Religions and the Evolution of Belief*. San Francisco: HarperOne.

_____ 2004. *Exploring the Religious Life*. Baltimore: Johns Hopkins University Press. Ch.6.

_____2003. *For the Glory of God: How Monotheism led to Reformations, Science, Witch-Hunts, and the End of Slavery*. Princeton: Princeton University Press.

_____1999a. "A Theory of Revelations," *Journal for the Scientific Study of Religion* 38(2):287-308.

_____ 1999b. "Micro Foundations of Religion: A Revised Theory," *Sociological Theory* 17(3):264-289.

Sun, Anna Xiao Dong. 2005. "The fate of Confucianism as a religion in socialist China: Controversies and paradoxes." In *State, Market and Religions in Chinese Societies* edited by Fenggang Yang and Joseph B. Tamney, pp. 229-51 (Leiden: Brill, 2005).

Tadros, Samuel. 2013. *Motherland Lost*. Stanford, CA: Hoover Institution.

Tobin, Gary A. and Aryeh K. Weinberg. 2007. *Profiles of the American University: Religious Beliefs and Behavior of College Faculty*. San Francisco: Institute for Jewish & Community Studies.

Wallace, Anthony F.C. 1966. *Religion: An Anthropological View*. New York: Random House.

Walter, Jess. 2002. *The Truth and Tragedy of the Randy Weaver Family*. New York: Harpers.

Watson, Leon. 2011. "The Arabic school textbooks which show children how to chop off hands and feet under Sharia law." *The Daily Mail*, December 23.

Watt, W. Montgomery. 1961. *Muhammad: Prophet and Statesman*. Oxford: Oxford University Press.

Williams, Michael Allen. 1996. *Rethinking "Gnosticism": An Argument for Dismantling a Dubious Category*. Princeton, Princeton University Press.

Wright, Lawrence. 2007. *The Looming Tower*. New York: Vintage Press.

Wright, Stuart A. 1995. *Armageddon in Waco*. Chicago: University of Chicago Press.

Index

1:25

1:30

1:35

1:45

2:00